JOURNEY TO FREEDOM

Growing Up TO BE President

Mary Carol Ghislin

Cover Photo Credit:

Focused Adventures;

(John Adams, 1793) National Portrait Gallery, Smithsonian Institution;

(Washington, 1783) National Portrait Gallery, Smithsonian Institution; gift of Katie Louchheim;

(Madison, c. 1801) National Portrait Gallery, Smithsonian Institution;

(Jefferson, 1786) National Portrait Gallery, Smithsonian Institution; bequest of Charles Francis Adams;

(c. 1818, Monroe) Smithsonian American Art Museum, Bequest of Mary Elizabeth Spencer

Cover and Book design by
Eric Dossou and Armando Lopez

Table of Contents

George Washington's Letter to the Hebrew Congregation

George Washington to the Hebrew Congregation in Newport, Rhode Island

Gentlemen.   [Newport, R.I., 18 August 1790]

While I receive, with much satisfaction, your Address replete with expressions of affection and esteem; I rejoice in the opportunity of assuring you, that I shall always retain a grateful remembrance of the cordial welcome I experienced in my visit to Newport, from all classes of Citizens.

The reflection on the days of difficulty and danger which are past is rendered the more sweet, from a consciousness that they are succeeded by days of uncommon prosperity and security. If we have wisdom to make the best use of the advantages with which we are now favored, we cannot fail, under the just administration of a good Government, to become a great and a happy people.

The Citizens of the United States of America have a right to applaud themselves for having given to mankind examples of an enlarged and liberal policy: a policy worthy of imitation. All possess alike liberty of conscience and immunities of citizenship. It is now no more that toleration is spoken of, as if it was by the indulgence of one class of people, that another enjoyed the exercise of their inherent natural rights. For happily the Government of the United States, which gives to bigotry no sanction, to persecution no assistance required only that they who live under its protection should demean themselves as good citizens, in giving it on all occasions their effectual support.

It would be inconsistent with the frankness of my character not to avow that I am pleased with your favorable opinion of my Administration, and fervent wishes for my felicity. May the Children of the Stock of Abraham, who dwell in this land, continue to merit and enjoy the good will of the other inhabitants; while every one shall sit in safety under his own vine and figtree, and there shall be none to make him afraid. May the father of all mercies scatter light and not darkness in our paths, and make us all in our several vocations useful here, and in his own due time and way everlastingly happy.

                                    Go: Washington

George Washington Primary Source Discussion

Read George Washington's letter to the Hebrew congregation, and then answer the questions below.

Close Reading and Careful Speaking

1. Who wrote this letter, and why was it written?

   ____

   ____

2. Was it written before or after the American Revolutionary War? What details in the letter give you this information?

   ____

   ____

3. Was this letter written to a private or to a public audience?

   ____

   ____

4. What does the author say about religious freedom in this letter?

   ____

   ____

5. Why might the congregation have chosen to write to George Washington with their question? Why not just write to the local sheriff?

   ____

   ____

> **Word Workout**
> - How many "expressions of affection" did George Washington receive from the congregation? What word expresses this?
>
> - "Felicity" means *happiness*. On what occasions might you extend wishes for someone's continued felicity?
>
> - *Demean* is a homonym. To demean someone comes from the adjective *mean* and describes making someone feel small. The other meaning of *demean* comes from the Anglo-French verb *demener*, which means *to conduct*. How does Washington want American citizens to behave?

George Washington Comprehension Questions

Read the essay in *Growing Up to Be President*, then answer the questions below.

1. **Knowledge** Why did George Washington not receive the education he expected?

2. **Knowledge** When Washington was appointed Commander-in-Chief of the Continental Army and first president, how many in Congress voted for him?

3. **Application** What early experiences might have made Washington so resilient and diligent?

4. **Comprehension** Washington cared a great deal about serving his nation. In what ways did he put the needs of his country before his own?

5. **Evaluation** Why do you think Washington thought he needed to work to keep the union together?

Word Workout

- How does the title of Washington's book, *Youths Behaviour*, give you a hint about the meaning of the word *civility*?

- What might a person have to do to be called "a person of distinction"?

- Can you think of a synonym for *resounding*?

- How might you show that you are competent in a job? If *incorrect* means *not correct*, then what might *incompetence* mean?

John Adams Comprehension Questions

Read the essay in *Growing Up to Be President*, then answer the questions below.

1. **Knowledge** What was John Adams eager to develop for himself, and whose writings inspired him to do it?

   ____

   ____

2. **Knowledge** What job did Adams have before turning to politics?

   ____

   ____

3. **Comprehension** In what ways did the Continental Congress make use of Adams' legal skills?

   ____

   ____

4. **Knowledge** What part of the government did Adams think needed strengthening?

   ____

   ____

5. **Analysis** As the first Minister to England, Adams had a unique insight on foreign policy. Yet when things became more hostile with France, a new challenge arose. What new aspect of foreign policy do you think Adams was forced to learn about?

   ____

   ____

Word Workout

- Can you name someone today who is *renowned*? What did that person do to earn it?

- What did attorney Adams say that provoked the British soldiers to fire?

- Why might a government worry about sedition?

American Minister John Adams Meets King George

John Adams arrived in London on May 26, 1785 as first United States Minister to Britain. He met with King George about one week later.

"I made the three Reverences, one at the Door, another about half Way and the third before the Presence, according to the Usage established at this and all the Northern Courts of Europe, and there addressed myself to his Majesty in the following Words—"

"Sir, The United States of America have appointed me their Minister Plenipotentiary to your Majesty…It is in Obedience to their express Commands that I have the Honor to assure your Majesty of their unanimous Disposition and Desire to cultivate the most friendly and liberal Intercourse between your Majesty's Subjects and their Citizens…The appointment of a Minister from the United States to your Majesty's Court, will form an Epocha in the History of English & of America. I think myself more fortunate than all my fellow Citizens in having the distinguished Honor to be the first to stand in your Majesty's Royal Presence in a diplomatic Character…"

Response of King George III (transcribed later by John Adams, to the best of his memory)

"I wish you Sir, to believe, and that it may be understood in America, that I have done nothing in the late Contest, but what I thought myself indispensably bound to do, by the duty which I owed to my People. I will be very frank with you. I was the last to consent to the Separation, but the Separation having been made and having become inevitable, I have always said, as I say now, that I would be the first to meet the Friendship of the United States as an independent Power…let the Circumstances of Language; Religion and Blood have their natural and full Effect."

Word Workout

- How many different meanings of *minister* might there be?

- *Pleni-* means full, and *potent* in the middle of the word means powerful. So what might be a *plenipotentiary*?

- What was King George referring to when he said "the late Contest"?

John Adams Primary Source Discussion

Close Reading and Careful Speaking

1. Why does Adams refer to the king as "the Presence"? What might this term indicate about Adams' and others' concept of the monarchy?

   ____

   ____

   ____

2. Why might it have been important for Adams to make the distinction between "your Majesty's subjects and their Citizens"? Who are the citizens? And who are the subjects?

   ____

   ____

   ____

3. Use your own words to explain what Adams meant when he said, "...will form an Epocha in the History of English & of America."

   ____

   ____

   ____

4. What tone do you read in King George's response? That is, what feeling seems to predominate as he speaks?

   ____

   ____

   ____

Weigh Your Ideas

What "natural and full effect" has happened to the relationship between Great Britain and America based on "Language; Religion and Blood"? Has King George's desire come to fruition?

Thomas Jefferson's Instructions to Meriwether Lewis

Primary Source

"To Meriwether Lewis, esquire, Captain of the 1st regiment of infantry of the United States of America.

"…Your mission has been communicated to the Ministers here from France, Spain, & Great Britain, and through them to their governments: and such assurances given them as to it's objects as we trust will satisfy them. The country of Louisiana having been ceded by Spain to France, the passport you have from the Minister of France, … will be a protection with all its subjects: and that from the Minister of England will entitle you to the friendly aid of any traders of that allegiance with whom you may happen to meet.

"The object of your mission is to explore the Missouri river, & such principal stream of it, as, by it's course & Communication with the water of the Pacific ocean may offer the most direct & practicable water communication across this continent, for the purposes of commerce….

"In all your intercourse with the natives[,] treat them in the most friendly & conciliatory manner which their own conduct will admit; allay all jealousies as to the object of your journey, satisfy them of it's innocence, make them acquainted with the position, extent, character, peaceable & commercial dispositions of the U.S., of our wish to be neighborly, friendly & useful to them, & of our dispositions to a commercial intercourse with them; confer with them on the points most convenient as mutual emporiums, & the articles of most desirable interchange for them & us. If a few of their influential chiefs, within practicable distance, wish to visit us, arrange such a visit with them, and furnish them with authority to call on our officers, on their entering the U.S. to have them conveyed to this place at the public expense. If any of them should wish to have some of their young people brought up with us, & taught such arts as may be useful to them, we will receive, instruct & take care of them. Such a mission, whether of influential chiefs, or of young people, would give some security to your own party. Carry with you some matter of the kine pox, inform those of them with whom you may be, of it's efficacy as a preservative from the small pox; and instruct & encourage them in the use of it. This may be especially done wherever you may winter…"

Thomas Jefferson Primary Source Discussion

Read Thomas Jefferson's instructions to Meriwether Lewis, and then answer the questions below.

Close Reading and Careful Speaking

1. Study the language of these instructions and decide whether they were given orally, or in writing. Explain your reasoning.

   ____

   ____

   ____

2. What does President Jefferson define as the object of the mission given to Meriwether Lewis? Find and quote his exact words.

   ____

   ____

   ____

3. In what context does President Jefferson use the word *emporiums*? What does he hope that the United States will do together with the natives?

   ____

   ____

   ____

Weigh Your Ideas

Does President Jefferson's concept of America's future with the native people seem plausible? Why or why not?

Word Workout

- How might the word *commercial* be connected to *commerce*? How can it help you understand what *commerce* means?

- The Middle English word *kye* meant *cows*. So if *kine* means *cow*, then what kind of medicine was President Jefferson sending along with the expedition?

- If President Jefferson wanted the expedition to treat the natives in a conciliatory manner, how did he want Americans to treat the natives? What clues can you find in the text to help you understand?

Thomas Jefferson Comprehension Questions

Read the essay in *Growing Up to Be President*, then answer the questions below.

1. **Knowledge** Which enslaved persons did Thomas Jefferson free after his death?

   ____

   ____

2. **Knowledge** Jefferson was reported to be a rather mediocre court lawyer but excelled in another area. Which part of the practice of law was he most recognized for?

   ____

   ____

3. **Knowledge** What purchase did Jefferson make that expanded the country's territory and secured trade routes?

   ____

   ____

4. **Evaluation** In what ways do you think Jefferson thought that a smaller government would benefit the farmers?

   ____

   ____

5. **Analysis** What part of Jefferson's childhood might have fostered his shy personality, and encouraged his confident and passionate writing?

   ____

   ____

Word Workout

- Under what conditions, other than the U.S. presidency, might you be asked to take an oath?

- What might Jefferson have had to do to commission all those explorers?

- What might be the difference between *traveling* and *traversing*?

What Are Checks and Balances?

Checks and balances are part of the system of the three branches of government that James Madison developed. The governmental responsibilities were divided among the branches so that no one branch could become too powerful. Moreover, each branch of the government has some power to influence the other branches, to "check" them to make sure they're staying in line, therefore, "balancing" the government's power structure.

The Executive branch—with the President at its head—can veto laws the Legislative branch passes (Congress), appoint judges, and extend pardons. The Judicial branch (the court system) can declare both presidential acts and laws passed by Congress to be unconstitutional. The Legislative branch (the House of Representatives and the Senate, or Congress) can impeach a president, overturn a veto with a two-thirds majority, and approve the appointments of judges.

The first meaningful test of this system was during John Tyler's presidency. Tyler vetoed two bills Congress passed that would establish a national bank. In turn, Congress gathered a two-thirds majority to overturn one of his vetoes. Then Congress impeached Tyler, although they did not vote to remove him from office. For many, it was a satisfying test of the new government's structure, which has remained intact to this day.

Close Reading and Careful Speaking

1. What are the three branches of the United States government?

   ____

   ____

2. Who developed the United States' system of government?

   ____

   ____

3. What is the purpose of checks and balances?

   ____

   ____

James Madison Comprehension Questions

Read the essay in *Growing Up to Be President*, then answer the questions below.

1. **Knowledge** What document did James Madison write that eventually became the basis for the constitution?

   ____

   ____

2. **Knowledge** Why was Madison a sickly child?

   ____

   ____

3. **Comprehension** How did Madison play to his strengths during his career?

   ____

   ____

4. **Evaluation** Which job prepared Madison most for his upcoming challenges with foreign affairs?

   ____

   ____

5. **Evaluation** Madison was a soft-spoken man but made tremendous impact on our governmental structure. What do you think gave him the confidence to fight for his beliefs?

   ____

   ____

Word Workout

- If Madison lost an election to someone who was more extroverted than he was, then how might his opponent have behaved?

- What do you think *coup de grace* means? Are there any clues in the text?

John Q. Adams and Thomas Jefferson React to the Missouri Compromise

John Quincy Adams wrote in his diary, 10 January 1820

"Take it for granted that the present is a mere preamble—a title page to a great, tragic volume...The President thinks this question will be winked away by a compromise—But so do not I—Much am I mistaken if it is not destined to survive his political and individual life and mine."

Jefferson, in a letter to Maine Representative John Holmes, April 22, 1820

"I had for a long time ceased to read newspapers or pay any attension to public affairs, confident they were in good hands, and content to be a passenger in our bark to the shore from which I am not distant. but this momentous question, like a fire bell in the night, awakened and filled me with terror. I considered it at once as the knell of the Union..."

Close Reading and Careful Speaking

1. Which president is John Quincy Adams referring to?

   ____

2. Put Adams' last sentence into your own words.

   ____

3. What reaction might be normal to a "fire bell in the night"?

   ____

Word Workout

- Paraphrase Adam's expression: "But so do not I."

- Jefferson's use of the word *bark* denotes a boat. This use is from the Latin word *barca*, meaning "small boat." Where is Jefferson talking about going?

- *Knell* comes from an Old English word *cynllan* which means to toll a bell. Is Jefferson expressing hope for the future of the Union?

James Monroe Comprehension Questions

Read the essay in *Growing Up to Be President*, then answer the questions below.

1. **Knowledge** During Monroe's term, what increased the tension between states that allowed slavery and those that didn't?

____

____

____

2. **Knowledge** Why do many historians think James Monroe was the most qualified person to ever hold the office of President?

____

____

____

3. **Knowledge** Why were some politicians hesitant to allow Missouri to join the union as a state that allowed slavery?

____

____

____

4. **Comprehension** What event was a challenge to the Era of Good Feelings?

____

____

____

5. **Analysis** What were the components of the Monroe Doctrine?

____

____

____

Word Workout

If you were to align yourself with a group at school, how might you signal your alignment?

John Quincy Adams Comprehension Questions

Read the essay in *Growing Up to Be President*, then answer the questions below.

1. **Knowledge** While his presidency did not bear much fruit, what other positions did John Quincy hold that left a profound impact on our government?

   ____

   ____

   ____

2. **Comprehension** What part of Adams' childhood might have prepared him most for his work in government?

   ____

   ____

   ____

3. **Knowledge** What subject did Adams continuously and passionately argue in Congress?

   ____

   ____

   ____

4. **Evaluation** Why do you think Adams was met with such fierce opposition as president?

   ____

   ____

   ____

Word Workout

- Do you have any interests that might be described as avid hobbies?

- What kinds of tasks might a diplomatic envoy be expected to do?

- What behavior in the Senate tells you what *eloquent* means?

Andrew Jackson Comprehension Questions

Read the essay in *Growing Up to Be President*, then answer the questions below.

1. **Knowledge** What was the name of the era of politics that Andrew Jackson ushered in?

   ____

   ____

2. **Knowledge** What was the Trail of Tears?

   ____

   ____

3. **Analysis** Jackson was mostly either loved or hated. What made him so controversial?

   ____

   ____

4. **Analysis** Why might it have been important for the Cherokee nation to develop their own government documents?

   ____

   ____

5. **Evaluation** What might have been important about President Jackson's rejection of the Supreme Court's decision?

   ____

   ____

Word Workout

- What does *aristocracy* mean? Where can you look in the text to help you find out?

- What was the difference between Jackson's gruff manor and the more traditionally educated presidents before him?

- How did Jackson act domineering?

"

Martin Van Buren Comprehension Questions

Read the essay in *Growing Up to Be President* and then answer the questions below.

1. **Comprehension** What was special about Van Buren's birth status compared to the previous presidents?

   ____

   ____

2. **Application** How did Van Buren show commitment to the American people during his legal career?

   ____

   ____

3. **Evaluation** If Van Buren lost the politicians' trust because he kept his own views secret, what should he have done instead to win votes and move up the political ladder?

   ____

   ____

4. **Knowledge** Did Martin Van Buren support a strong centralized government, or individual state's supremacy?

   ____

   ____

5. **Knowledge** What system did Van Buren spend three years trying to convince Congress to support?

   ____

   ____

Word Workout

- How did Van Buren utilize his family connections?

- How might someone act with vigor? What part of the text helps you understand this?

The Bank War

During George Washington's presidency, Alexander Hamilton proposed a federal financial system with a national bank to hold government funds and issue money. It would uniformly support business across state lines and international trade.

Yet not everyone agreed. Thomas Jefferson and James Madison believed that it would give the federal government too much power, harming the rural landowners. Over this issue, Hamilton and Jefferson formed opposing political parties: the Federalist and Democratic-Republican parties. In the end, Congress accepted Hamilton's idea, and President Washington signed it into law in 1791, with a twenty-year charter, which expired in 1811.

Three years later in 1814, James Madison, on Jefferson's side initially, now decided that another national bank was necessary because of the expensive War of 1812. The 2nd National Bank also had a twenty-year charter. These banks were successful, but when the time came again to renew the charter, Andrew Jackson was president. He had a deep mistrust of banks and paper money. But while Congress approved the bank charter's renewal, Jackson vetoed it, and Congress was one vote short of the two-thirds majority needed to override it.

President Martin Van Buren had always agreed with Jackson, but during Van Buren's presidency, the nation faced its worst economic crisis yet—The Panic of 1837. Many of the state banks' reserves were running low. Fearing their money would soon be worthless, people stopped doing business. The economy was in shambles. Van Buren called a special session of Congress and proposed an independent national treasury—contrary to his early Jacksonian beliefs. Congress passed it into law in 1840.

Close Reading and Careful Speaking

1. Who were the three presidents who signed charters for the national bank?

____

____

William H. Harrison Comprehension Questions

Read the essay in *Growing Up to Be President*, then answer the questions below.

1. **Knowledge** William Henry Harrison wanted to build fame. So what was his first step toward the recognition he craved?

   ____

   ____

   ____

2. **Evaluation** How might Harrison's childhood have informed his desire for fame?

   ____

   ____

   ____

3. **Knowledge** What did Harrison do to gain popularity in the Northwest Territory?

   ____

   ____

   ____

4. **Evaluation** Why do you suppose Harrison lost most of his political campaigns?

   ____

   ____

   ____

5. **Evaluation** What personality trait do you think may have led to Harrison's untimely death?

   ____

   ____

   ____

Word Workout

- If you had to initiate a procedure for starting a new club, what steps might you take?

- Why might it not have been ethical for Governor Harrison to take charge of troops after a thirteen-year absence from the army?

- If a news story reported on the demise of a business, what happened to the business?

John Tyler Comprehension Questions

Read the essay in *Growing Up to Be President*, then answer the questions below.

1. **Anaysis** What aspect of Tyler's upbringing likely gave him the status and connections he needed to comfortably start his career?

   ____

   ____

2. **Knowledge** On the issue of states' rights versus a powerful central government, which side did Tyler take?

   ____

   ____

3. **Knowledge** What important precedent did Tyler set when he took office?

   ____

   ____

4. **Knowledge** Tyler was not popular. But his unpopularity gave Congress an opportunity to test some systems that had not been used before. Which were they?

   ____

   ____

5. **Comprehension** What message about the presidency did Congress project while Tyler was in office?

   ____

   ____

Word Workout

- A *precedent* is an event that serves as a model for future events. What advantage might there be to following precedents?

- Would a politician who had been impeached be able to continue serving in his office?

James K. Polk Comprehension Questions

Read the essay in *Growing Up to Be President*, then answer the questions below.

1. **Knowledge** Which president was James K. Polk's mentor?

2. **Synthesis** What did Polk and his mentor have in common?

3. **Application** What personal quality did Polk have that helped advance his political career?

4. **Knowledge** What was the reason for the Mexican-American War?

5. **Analysis** The tension between the slave and free states grew considerably during Polk's time in office. What were some of the reasons for that?

Word Workout

- What kind of a job might you have that might require a mentor?

- To *abide* means to wait or stay. So if you bide your time, what are you doing?

- What clues in the text tell you what *contrarian* means?

The War of 1812

With the Louisiana Purchase money in their pockets, France declared war on Great Britain. At first, the United States was able to continue doing business with both warring parties through international sea trade. But each side wanted the United States to stop trading with the other, and consequently, American ships were continually attacked by both countries.

Moreover, Britain had a problem with hundreds of their sailors deserting by jumping ship onto American ships. To arrest them, the British boarded American ships, conveniently enacting a policy of impressment. This meant that the British searched American civilian ships for deserters and forcefully brought them back to the British Navy, including many innocent Americans. In 1807, President Jefferson signed the Embargo Act, ceasing all trade with both countries. In just a few months, the American economy was suffering immeasurably.

The British later apologized for their behavior. To complicate matters, Americans were facing increasing tension with Native Americans. To maintain their trade and economy, the British had been selling weapons to the natives, who were growing more worried about American westward expansion. To solve at least the slowdown in the economy, in 1809, President Madison signed the Non-Intercourse Act, which jumpstarted American trade with every country *except* France and Great Britain.

In response, Britain and France created tit-for-tat laws that blockaded American trade from the other, making it extremely dangerous for American ships to trade. Over the next few years, the United States struggled to regain their trading economy, until in 1812, after a very close vote in both the House and the Senate, Congress declared war on Great Britain.

Close Reading and Careful Speaking

1. Why might France have waited to declare war on Great Britain until after they had sold the Louisiana territory?

   ____

   ____

Zachary Taylor and Millard Fillmore Comprehension Questions

Read the essays in *Growing Up to Be President*, then answer the questions below.

1. **Comprehension** How did Zachary Taylor show humanity during his time in the military?

   ____

   ____

2. **Comprehension** Why might Taylor have kept his political views secret while he was a soldier?

   ____

   ____

3. **Evaluation** How might President Taylor's support of the Clayton-Bulwer Treaty be related to his respect for Native Americans?

   ____

   ____

4. **Application** In his childhood, how did Millard Fillmore express persistence?

   ____

   ____

5. **Evaluation** Why might young Millard's father have taken so long to see that he was interested in learning?

   ____

   ____

6. **Application** What aspects of Fillmore's childhood may have affected his work in the New York state legislature?

   ____

   ____

7. **Comprehension** Why did no one feel satisfied by the Compromise of 1850?

   ____

   ____

Franklin Pierce Comprehension Questions

Read the essay in *Growing Up to Be President*, then answer the questions below.

1. **Knowledge** What was important to Franklin Pierce both as a young person and as a politician?

   ____

   ____

   ____

2. **Knowledge** Why was Pierce popular among southern legislators?

   ____

   ____

   ____

3. **Comprehension** Why was it important that presidential candidate Pierce did not have a national reputation?

   ____

   ____

   ____

4. **Knowledge** What was the name of the bill Pierce passed that led to "Bleeding Kansas," and why did violence break out because of it?

   ____

   ____

   ____

Word Workout

- How did Franklin Pierce's father garner respect from the local citizens?

- Latitudes are geographical measurements that are marked on globes. Study a globe or a map. What is the difference between latitude and longitude?

James Buchanan Comprehension Questions

Read the essay in *Growing Up to Be President*, then answer the questions below.

1. **Evauation** What in James Buchanan's childhood may have led to his rowdiness in college?

2. **Knowledge** Which two countries was Buchanan an ambassador for?

3. **Knowledge** What was Buchanan's position on slavery?

4. **Analysis** Why was it a benefit to Buchanan that he had been overseas during much of Congress' arguing over slavery?

5. **Application** Assess President-elect Buchanan's actions to influence the Supreme Court decision in the Dred Scott case. Do they align with his stated faith in the judicial system?

> **Word Workout**
> - Describe how you might feel if a job eludes you.
> - With the announcement of the Supreme Court decision in the Dred Scott case, Southerners felt vindicated. In your own words, describe how they felt.

Abraham Lincoln Comprehension Questions

Read the essay in *Growing Up to Be President*, then answer the questions below.

1. **Anlysis** Lincoln argued legal cases in court before he earned his license, while he was still studying the law. What might this say about his character?

____

2. **Knowledge** What was one of Abraham Lincoln's qualities that made even members of the opposing party vote for him?

____

3. **Knowledge** What political idea of Steven Douglas did Lincoln challenge as the most dangerous threat to American democracy during his campaign for the U.S. Senate?

____

4. **Comprehension** Discuss the difference between the words *legal* and *moral* that President Lincoln made during the early days of his presidency.

____

5. **Analysis** Outline the steps President Lincoln took at the outset of the war, and national circumstances, that led him to finally issue the Emancipation Proclamation.

____

6. **Evaluation** Interpret President Abraham Lincoln's actions and name personal qualities that they demonstrated.

____

> **Word Workout**
>
> - Have you ever been a member of a club or a team, in two consecutive years? How do you know they were consecutive?
>
> - When Southern states seceded from the Union, what exactly did they do?
>
> - If the word *imprisonment* is the opposite of *emancipation*, then what does *emancipation* mean?

The National Banking System

The Civil War quickly grew to a scope well beyond what people initially imagined. Instead of a quick skirmish, it had turned into a long, hard slog, requiring the government to spend more money. Quickly going from a budget surplus to a huge deficit, Congress decided it was time to give national banking another try.

One of the problems the federal government ran into was that most money in circulation was in the form of coins and notes issued by state banks. So most of the time, the state banks would only accept other states' currency at a discount, if at all. This meant that a dollar issued by the state of Georgia might have been worth less when the user tried to buy something in Florida.

This situation made doing business across state lines quite challenging. Because the Union government needed more money to finance the war, they decided to charter national banks and raise taxes on the state currencies to increase demand for the national currency.

The government then used these nationally chartered banks to sell government bonds. These are promissory notes that sell at one price and then later the government buys them back at a higher price. And because they were under the jurisdiction of the federal government, they were able to regulate them through the new Office of the Comptroller of the Currency. These banks set in place many systems that served as the foundation for the modern banking system to come.

Close Reading and Careful Speaking

1. What is a government bond and why might a government buy and sell them?

   ____

   ____

2. Why do you think state banks did not want to accept other states' notes?

   ____

   ____

Excerpt from Abraham Lincoln's Second Inaugural Address, March 4, 1865

"Fellow countrymen: … On the occasion corresponding to this four years ago all thoughts were anxiously directed to an impending civil war. All dreaded it…all sought to avert it… Both parties deprecated war but one of them would make war rather than let the nation survive, and the other would accept war rather than let it perish. And the war came.

"One eighth of the whole population were colored slaves … localized in the southern part of it. These slaves constituted a peculiar and powerful interest. All knew that this interest was somehow the cause of the war. To strengthen[,] perpetuate[,] and extend this interest was the object for which the insurgents would rend the Union even by war[,] while the government claimed no right to do more than to restrict the territorial enlargement of it… Neither anticipated that the cause of the conflict might cease with or even before the conflict itself should cease… Both read the same Bible and pray to the same God[,] and each invokes His aid against the other. It may seem strange that any men should dare to ask a just God's assistance in wringing their bread from the sweat of other men's faces[,] but let us judge not that we be not judged. The prayers of both could not be answered…that of neither has been answered fully. The Almighty has His own purposes. "Woe unto the world because of offenses[,] for it must needs be that offenses come[,] but woe to that man by whom the offense cometh." If we shall suppose that American slavery is one of those offenses[,] which in the providence of God must needs come[,] but which having continued through His appointed time He now wills to remove[,] and that He gives to both North and South this terrible war as the woe due to those by whom the offense came[,] shall we discern therein any departure from those divine attributes which the believers in a living God always ascribe to Him[?] Fondly do we hope…fervently do we pray… that this mighty scourge of war may speedily pass away. Yet, if God wills that it continue until all the wealth piled by the bondsman's two hundred and fifty years of unrequited toil shall be sunk[,] and until every drop of blood drawn with the lash shall be paid by another drawn with the sword[,] as was said three thousand years ago so still it must be said[,] 'the judgments of the Lord are true and righteous altogether.'

"With malice toward none[,] with charity for all[,] with firmness in the right as God gives us to see the right[,] let us strive on to finish the work we are in to bind up the nation's wounds, to care for him who shall have borne the battle and for his widow and his orphan…to do all which may achieve and cherish a just and lasting peace among ourselves and with all nations."

Abraham Lincoln Primary Source Discussion

Close Reading and Careful Speaking

1. On what occasion was Abraham Lincoln delivering this speech?

2. What was the state of the nation during this speech?

3. Whom was the speaker addressing?

4. What is Lincoln referring to when he says: "Neither anticipated that the cause of the conflict might cease with or even before the conflict itself should cease."?

5. Express in your own words what the speaker meant when he said, "Yet, if God wills..." to the end of that sentence.

Weigh Your Ideas

What elements in Lincoln's speech might indicate that the speech was delivered in a different time period?

Word Workout

- How might the word *surge* give you a clue for the meaning of the word *insurgent*?

- The Latin word *deprecari* means to attempt to prevent something by begging through prayer. Describe in your own words what each of the two sides in the country were doing, as Lincoln discussed it in the second paragraph?

- In what way might war be explained as a scourge?

Andrew Johnson Comprehension Questions

Read the essay in *Growing Up to Be President*, then answer the questions below.

1. **Analysis** Why might Andrew Johnson's childhood have led him to identify more with the southern tradesmen than the southern planters?

2. **Knowledge** What task was Johnson left with when he took over the presidency after the death of Lincoln?

3. **Knowledge** How did Johnson try to appease the southern planters?

4. **Comprehension** Why were Johnson's actions counterproductive to the reconstruction effort?

Word Workout

- Can you think of words that would be synonyms for *elite*? What would be antonyms for *elite*?

- Why might the job of pulling the country back together again have been excruciating?

- Have you ever experienced a reconciliation with someone? What did it look like?

Ulysses S. Grant Comprehension Questions

Read the essay in *Growing Up to Be President*, then answer the questions below.

1. **Comprehension** What events led to Ulysses S. Grant joining the military?

2. **Knowledge** What title did Grant hold that only George Washington had held before?

3. **Knowledge** What was Grant's top priority after becoming president?

4. **Synthesis** In what way did Grant show consistency in his attitude toward oppressed people?

> **Word Workout**
> A *siege* is a military maneuver in which a place is cut off from supplies or help.
> What moves would an army during the Civil War have made to lay siege to a city?

Rutherford B. Hayes Comprehension Questions

Read the essay in *Growing Up to Be President*, then answer the questions below.

1. **Analysis** Describe how Hayes was able to overcome the challenges in his childhood.

   ____

   ____

   ____

2. **Knowledge** Which amendments to the constitution did Rutherford B. Hayes support?

   ____

   ____

   ____

3. **Knowledge** What allowed southern legislators to break their promise to preserve the rights of the previously enslaved population?

   ____

   ____

   ____

4. **Synthesis** Provide an example of Hayes' behavior that mirrored George Washington's and describe the public's reaction to it.

   ____

   ____

   ____

Word Workout

- What conditions made Hayes refuse to electioneer for a seat in Congress?

- Why was the Compromise of 1877 described as one of the murkiest deals in history?

- How might historians express their consensus over a particular point of view?

"

James A. Garfield Comprehension Questions

Read the essay in *Growing Up to Be President*, then answer the questions below.

1. **Knowledge** What were young Garfield's two attempts to leave the farm, and how did each of them go?

   ____

   ____

   ____

2. **Knowledge** James A. Garfield did not spend long in the President's office but had a considerable career in Congress. What did he fight for in Congress?

   ____

   ____

   ____

3. **Analysis** Why might President Garfield's appointment to the Port of New York have been a disappointment to many historians?

   ____

   ____

   ____

4. **Evaluation** What reasons might someone have had to want Garfield out of office?

   ____

   ____

   ____

Word Workout

- Why might it be important to be sincere in one's actions?

- What does an abolitionist do? How might the essay on James Garfield help you figure it out?

- What might you do if you wanted to become aligned with a certain group?

Jim Crow Laws and Variants

Info Graphic

After the Civil War, white Southerners were able to pass laws that segregated newly freed Black Americans. The laws were called Jim Crow, after a Black American minstrel routine.

Schools separated by race	Alabama, Florida, Georgia, Louisiana, Mississippi	Missouri, New Mexico, North Carolina, South Carolina, Texas	Yet, New Orleans had integrated schools
Libraries provided for white and black patrons as separate buildings	North Carolina	Texas	
Anyone who promoted equality was fined $500	Mississippi	But in North Carolina, Black Americans were allowed to serve on juries with whites.	
Railroads had separate cars for white and black customers.	Alabama	Maryland, Virginia	Same laws in New York, but were struck down in a case defended by Chester Arthur.
Law required separations in barbers, buses, restaurants, theaters, housing, parks.	Alabama, Georgia	Louisiana, South Carolina	Virginia

Interpreting Info Graphics

1. What law discouraged even white Americans from supporting changes to Jim Crow laws?

   ____

2. What one city had integrated schools, even during the Jim Crow era?

   ____

3. What Northern city also had segregated rail cars? What was the outcome of a lawsuit against that railroad company?

   ____

4. What public entertainment spaces were segregated?

   ____

Chester A. Arthur Comprehension Questions

Read the essay in *Growing Up to Be President*, then answer the questions below.

1. **Synthesis** How did Chester A. Arthur earn his nickname, and why might it have been so surprising?

   ____

   ____

   ____

2. **Knowledge** How did Arthur get recommended for the Vice President position?

   ____

   ____

   ____

3. **Knowledge** Which bill did Arthur sign that surprised Congress, given how he came into the presidency?

   ____

   ____

   ____

4. **Comprehension** In what ways did Arthur serve as a fulcrum leading the country into the modern era?

   ____

   ____

   ____

Word Workout

- What kinds of qualities, or events, might make an institution prestigious?

- If a President gives someone a patronage job, what is implied about their relationship?

What Is a Political Machine?

Commonly during the nineteenth century, local city governments were inefficient and therefore ineffective. It was hard to get things done. This culture of inefficiency allowed organizations called "political machines" to come into power. A political machine was an organization that controlled every part of the political process.

They would run elections, choose the candidates, make appointments for public positions, and then puppeteer politicians, once they took office. Since the machine had the power to remove someone from their office, the government officials had to do their bidding to keep their jobs. They would also often accept bribes from organized crime syndicates to look away from the machine's illegal activities.

One of the most powerful was called Tammany Hall and was based in New York City. The main goal of a political machine was to keep itself in power, not necessarily to do good public service, and this was true for Tammany Hall. As corrupt as this type of system was, people generally accepted them because, at the very least, things got done. It was just accepted as the way things were. Eventually, political reformers passed laws to correct these organizations built for bribery, and the political machine systems faded away.

Close Reading and Careful Speaking

1. Given what a political machine was, do you think the name is accurate?

____

____

____

2. What were some ways political machines were able to maintain power?

____

____

____

3. If political machines "got things done" then why were they a bad thing?

____

____

____

Grover Cleveland Comprehension Questions

Read the essay in *Growing Up to Be President*, then answer the questions below.

1. **Synthesis** How did Grover Cleveland put the needs of his family before his own, and how might his political career have been a result of that?

   ____

   ____

   ____

2. **Knowledge** What attitude did Cleveland take when he assumed the presidency?

   ____

   ____

   ____

3. **Knowledge** What major action did Cleveland take that contradicted his view that the government shouldn't intervene with social issues?

   ____

   ____

   ____

4. **Evaluation** If Cleveland was a reformer, why would his desire for reform not be enough to qualify him as a visionary?

   ____

   ____

   ____

> **Word Workout**
> - If Grover Cleveland served two non-consecutive terms, what would he have had to do to serve two consecutive terms?
>
> - In what ways are the words *corrupt* and *fraudulent* connected?
>
> - The prefix *inter-* can mean *between*. So if you were to intervene in an argument, what might you be doing?

Benjamin Harrison Comprehension Questions

Read the essay in *Growing Up to Be President*, then answer the questions below.

1. **Knowledge** Why was Benjamin Harrison called, "the human iceberg"?

   ____

   ____

   ____

2. **Synthesis** How did Harrison show his position on civil rights during his time as president?

   ____

   ____

   ____

3. **Application** With Benjamin Harrison's legacy and his apparent interest in the law, what other careers might he have pursued besides politics?

   ____

   ____

   ____

> **Word Workout**
> - *Mediocre* may come from the Latin word *medius*, meaning *middle*. Is this a fair word to describe the presidency of Benjamin Harrison?
> - When might it be appropriate for you to engage vigorously in an effort?

William McKinley Comprehension Questions

Read the essay in *Growing Up to Be President*, then answer the questions below.

1. **Knowledge** What impact did William McKinley have on public speaking in the White House?

   ____

   ____

   ____

2. **Knowledge** How did McKinley try to help the oppressed black population in the South?

   ____

   ____

   ____

3. **Synthesis** Why might McKinley not have been able to pass laws that supported Black Americans?

   ____

   ____

   ____

4. **Comprehension** Why did McKinley need to decide on a standard for the country's finances, and what was the decision he made?

   ____

   ____

   ____

> **Word Workout**
> - Describe a skill that you have that could be described as *competent*.
> - What synonym might be used for *precedent* in certain cases?

Theodore Roosevelt Comprehension Questions

Read the essay in *Growing Up to Be President*, then answer the questions below.

1. **Knowledge** How did young Roosevelt overcome his childhood struggles?

   ____

   ____

2. **Knowledge** Roosevelt made fairness a point in his negotiations, calling the result a Square Deal. But which group of people did that notion not necessarily include?

   ____

   ____

   ____

3. **Knowledge** What idea about government did Roosevelt have that was the first of its kind?

   ____

   ____

   ____

4. **Analysis** What qualities led Roosevelt to be popular with the people, but may have placed him at odds with the government? And why might government officials have felt threatened by him?

   ____

   ____

   ____

5. **Synthesis** How might Roosevelt's childhood travel have influenced his outlook during his presidency?

   ____

   ____

   ____

> ### Word Workout
>
> - How can you describe what an extrovert is like?
>
> - If the ancient Greek word *philein* means *to love*, and the word *anthropos* means *humankind*, what might the word *philanthropist* mean? What might a philanthropist do?

Theodore Roosevelt and National Parks

President Theodore Roosevelt signed six national parks into law. Later, Congress gave all presidents the power to proclaim National Monuments without congressional approval. The Antiquities Act of 1906, allowed any President to "declare by public proclamation historic landmarks, historic and prehistoric structures, ...to be National Monuments."

National Monuments	National Parks	Monuments That Became National Parks
Devil's Tower (WY), 1906	Crater Lake National Park (OR), 1902	Petrified Forest (AZ), 1906
El Morrow (NM), 1906	Wind Cave National Park (SD), 1903	Lassen Peak and Cinder Cone, now Lassen Volcanic National Park, (CA), 1907
Montezuma Castle (AZ), 1906	Sullys Hill (ND), 1904	Grand Canyon (AZ), 1908
Chaco Canyon (NM), 1907	Platt National Park (OK), 1906	Pinnacles (CA), 1908
Gila Cliff Dwellings (NM), 1907	Mesa Verde National Park (CO), 1906	Wheeler (CO), 1908
Tonto (AZ), 1907	Enlarged Yosemite National Park (CA), 1864	Mount Olympus (WA), 1909, now Olympic National Park
Muir Woods (CA), 1908		
Jewel Cave (SD), 1908		
Natural Bridges (UT), 1908		
Tumacacori (AZ), 1908		

Interpreting Info Graphics

1. Which national park did President Roosevelt add on to, but did not establish?

____

2. Which two states have an equal number of monuments founded by President Roosevelt?

____

3. In which region of the country did President Roosevelt establish four national parks?

____

William H. Taft Comprehension Questions

Read the essay in *Growing Up to Be President*, then answer the questions below.

1. **Analysis** Who convinced Taft to go into politics, and how did his lack of interest in the political system show?

   ____

   ____

   ____

2. **Application** What foreign country benefited most from Taft's judicial expertise?

   ____

   ____

   ____

3. **Knowledge** What did Taft promise before taking the office of President, and did he keep that promise?

   ____

   ____

   ____

4. **Comprehension** How did the controversy around Taft affect his campaign for re-election?

   ____

   ____

   ____

> **Word Workout**
>
> The Supreme Court writes two papers on every ruling they make. One paper explains the majority opinion, and the second paper explains the minority opinion. Which one is the dissenting option?

The Federal Reserve Act, 1913

Although the banking acts of 1863 and 1864 had positively supported the economy, they were not perfect. In the late 1800s, while the United States was experiencing economic growth, no less than eight banking panics affected cities along the East Coast, while three others affected the entire nation. These were characterized by people making "runs" on banks, which means they were worried their bank would fail, so customers in the hundreds withdrew their deposits, further weakening the bank. After each panic, talk of financial reform came up, but Congress didn't act until after the panic of 1907. Finally, they assigned a committee to research financial reform.

In addition, executives in the banking industry also desired reform and secretly met to put together their own plan, fearing that the public wouldn't trust a plan that came from bankers. They worked intensively and secretly for about a week and then presented it to Congress. Their plan was not immediately accepted, but a few years later, it was used as the basis for the Federal Reserve Act and was passed into law.

The new Federal Reserve Bank had the authority to increase and decrease the supply of cash in circulation, which gave American currency the "elasticity" that it lacked before. The new structure also allowed banks to quickly turn assets into cash, which they would need if many people began withdrawing at once. The act has been revised several times since its inception, but the system remains in place today.

1. Why would people want to withdraw their deposits if they thought their bank was going to fail?

   ____

   ____

2. Why might banking panics make the government think that something needed to be fixed?

   ____

   ____

3. Why might people not trust a bank reform plan that came from bankers themselves?

   ____

   ____

Woodrow Wilson Comprehension Questions

Read the essay in *Growing Up to Be President*, then answer the questions below.

1. **Application** How might young Woodrow's Civil War experience have shaped his perception of the whole country when he stepped into the Presidency?

   ____

   ____

2. **Knowledge** How did Woodrow Wilson surprise the political machine bosses that recommended him for office?

   ____

   ____

3. **Application** Wilson was the first President from the South since the end of the Civil War. What characteristics of the South did he bring with him?

   ____

   ____

4. **Knowledge** What was the most controversial law he signed during World War I, and what did it do?

   ____

   ____

5. **Analysis** How did Wilson break the previous tradition around the relationship between the president and Congress?

   ____

   ____

6. **Knowledge** How did Wilson help the war effort?

   ____

   ____

> **Word Workout**
> - What does *neutrality* mean? How does the text help you figure it out?
> - Identify a small word inside the word *formative*. How can it help you decide what *formative* means?

The Cost of World War I

Info Graphic

Approximate Cost, in Billions of Dollars Courtesy Library of Congress		
Total Cost, *approximate*	Includes money spent on uniforms, weapons, munitions, transportation, communications, food, and all equipment needed.	$24,620,000,000
Credits to eleven nations	Includes loans made to allies who used the money to purchase supplies for the war effort.	$8,841,657,000
Taxes paid by the American people in 1918	This is the portion of American tax dollars allocated to the war.	$3,694,000,000
Money raised by selling Liberty Loans	The U.S. government asked Americans to "loan" them money, which the government paid back to them with interest.	$14,000,000,000
War Savings Stamps to November, 1918	The government sold 10-cent stamps that collectors placed in books.	$834,253,000

Interpreting Info Graphics

Study the information in the table to answer the questions below.

1. To extend "credit" means that you lend money to someone. So why might the United States government have loaned money to its allies? What advantage would there be to our war effort to do that?

   ____

   ____

2. What might be the purpose in selling inexpensive stamps to collectors? How could such small amounts help the war effort?

   ____

   ____

Warren G. Harding Comprehension Questions

Read the essay in *Growing Up to Be President*, then answer the questions below.

1. **Knowledge** What business venture put Harding on the radar of politicians?

2. **Synthesis** What quality about Warren G. Harding was both one of his best and worst attributes?

3. **Knowledge** What was Harding's presidency most remembered for?

4. **Comprehension** Harding viewed the presidency as a mostly ceremonial position. What are some of his actions that reflected that attitude?

Work Workout

- In what way is corruption like rust on an engine?

- What clues in the text could help you understand the meaning of *defrauding*?

Calvin Coolidge Comprehension Questions

Read the essay in *Growing Up to Be President*, then answer the questions below.

1. **Knowledge** What was Calvin Coolidge's attitude toward the presidency?

   ____

   ____

   ____

2. **Knowledge** What did Coolidge say in response to a strike by the Boston police that made national headlines?

   ____

   ____

   ____

3. **Comprehension** How might Coolidge have been inspired to pursue a life in politics?

   ____

   ____

   ____

4. **Synthesis** Compare how Coolidge acted during his presidency and during his time holding other public offices.

   ____

   ____

   ____

Word Workout

- What words in the text help you understand what *manifold* means?

- If pivot means to turn on a central point, what might *pivotal* mean?

- If farmers during the 1920s wanted to be subsidized by the federal government, what exactly might they have wanted?

Herbert Hoover Comprehension Questions

Read the essay in *Growing Up to Be President*, then answer the questions below.

1. **Knowledge** What government positions did Herbert Hoover hold before he became president?

   ____

   ____

   ____

2. **Knowledge** Which major economic event started during Hoover's term?

   ____

   ____

   ____

3. **Evaluation** Do you think Hoover's humanitarian tendencies would have been different had his childhood circumstances been better?

   ____

   ____

   ____

4. **Comprehension** Why have historians decided that Hoover wasn't a very good politician?

   ____

   ____

   ____

Word Workout

- What two smaller words make up the word *lackluster*? How can they tell you what *lackluster* means?

- Knowing that statistics describe numbers, how might statistics be useful to politicians?

- The word *sociologist* has the word *social* in it. How can that help you understand what kind of scientist a sociologist is?

Statistics on the Great Depression

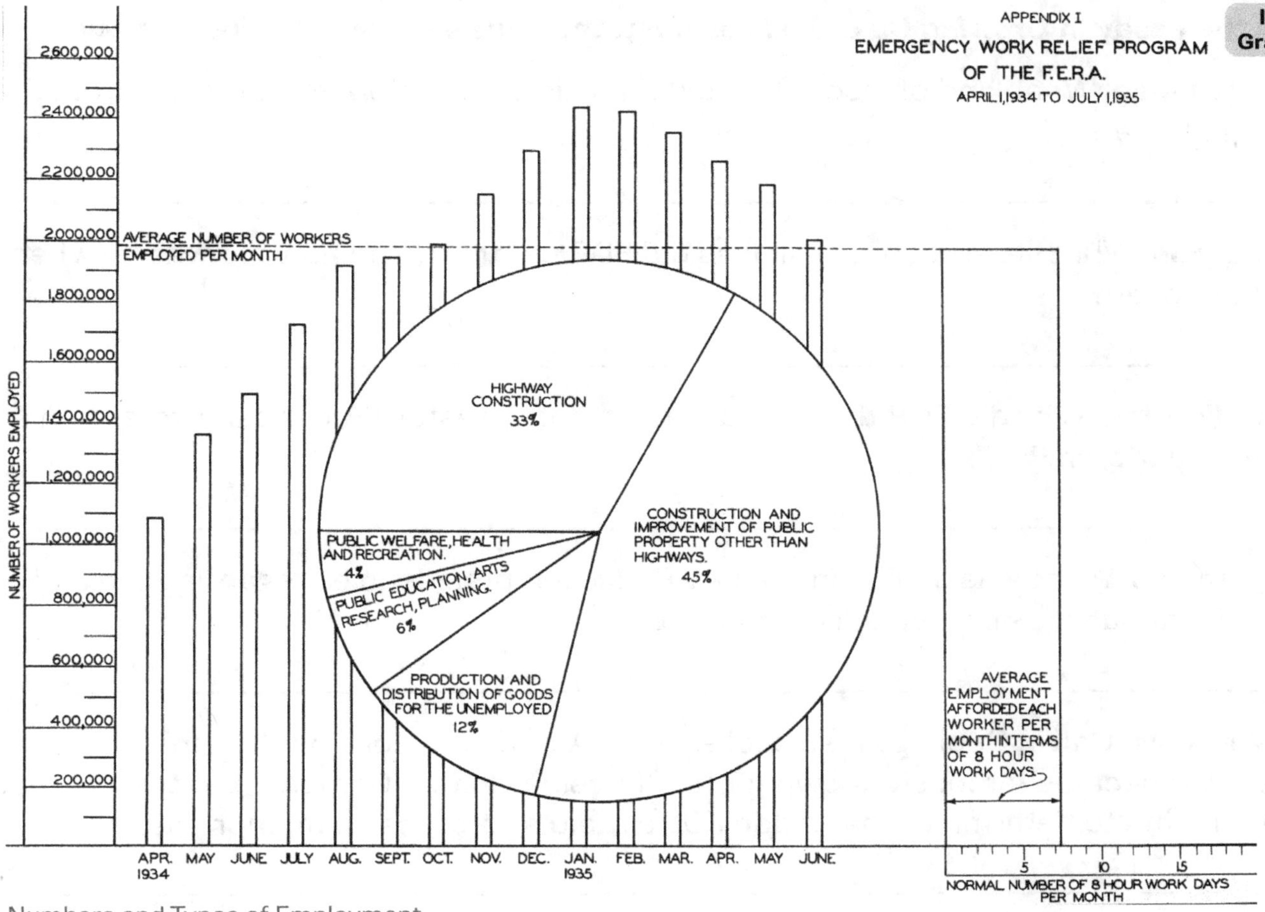

Numbers and Types of Employment

Interpreting Info Graphics

1. For each American on the work-relief program, how many days each month did he or she work?

   ____

2. In January of 1935, about how many more workers were employed than were able to work in April of 1934?

   ____

3. What percentage of workers were employed in highway construction?

   ____

4. What were most employees doing?

   ____

5. What kinds of jobs might have been part of the category called "Public Welfare, Health, and Recreation"?

   ____

Franklin Delano Roosevelt Comprehension Questions

Read the essay in *Growing Up to Be President*, then answer the questions below.

1. **Knowledge** What kind of inspiration did Franklin Delano Roosevelt receive from a distant relative?

   ____

2. **Analysis** What life-threatening illness did FDR contract, and how old was he when it happened?

   ____

3. **Application** Why did FDR think it was important to restore Americans' trust in the banking system?

   ____

4. **Synthesis** What was similar in the two Roosevelt presidencies regarding their beliefs about the purpose of government?

   ____

5. **Synthesis** Calvin Coolidge also spoke to the American public on the radio, yet FDR became famously known for his "Fireside Chats." Compare the two Presidents to determine what made FDR's radio addresses so memorable.

   ____

> **Word Workout**
> - If the word *curriculum* describes all the teaching and learning that happens in class, what kinds of activities might be extracurricular?
>
> - What qualities in a nurse would FDR have needed to help him survive polio? Describe how a nurse might be staunch.
>
> - If ammunition describes the bullets that are used in weapons, what might munitions refer to?

Franklin Delano Roosevelt and World War II

> Excerpt from the President's message to Congress, delivered on December 8, 1941
>
> "Yesterday, December 7, 1941—a date which will live in infamy—the United States of America was suddenly and deliberately attacked by naval and air forces of the Empire of Japan.
>
> "The United States was at the moment at peace with that nation and at the solicitation of Japan was still in conversation with its Government and its Emperor looking toward the maintenance of peace in the Pacific...
>
> "I, therefore, ask that the Congress declare that since the unprovoked ... attack by Japan on Sunday, December seventh, a state of war has existed between the United States and the Japanese Empire."

Close Reading and Careful Speaking

1. **Evaluation** What might have happened if FDR hadn't loosened the country's commitment to neutrality before Pearl Harbor was attacked?

   ____

   ____

2. **Knowledge** What was the name of the head of the Japanese government?

   ____

   ____

3. **Comprehension** What is President Roosevelt asking Congress to do?

   ____

   ____

Word Workout

- The word *infamy* is related to the word *famous*. But the prefix *in-* changes the meaning in the same way that *incorrect* is related to *correct*. So what does *infamy* mean?

- How does FDR think that everyone will remember this date?

Harry S. Truman Comprehension Questions

Read the essay in *Growing Up to Be President*, then answer the questions below.

1. **Analysis** How were Harry Truman's professional ventures related, and how might they have prepared him for office?

   ____

   ____

   ____

2. **Knowledge** What decision did Truman make that brought about the end of World War II?

   ____

   ____

   ____

3. **Knowledge** Why have historians' opinions on Truman softened over the years?

   ____

   ____

   ____

4. **Evaluation** Why do you think Truman was unpopular as he left office?

   ____

   ____

   ____

Word Workout

- Lynching was a form of punishment carried out before the benefit of a trial. Although it occurred in England and colonial America, it became common across the South after the Civil War. What effect might widespread lynching have on a population?

- If young Harry's mother would not let him play strenuously, what might it mean that he was not a robust boy?

- The word part *infra-* means *below*, or *beneath*. What then might *infrastructure* mean?

Dwight D. Eisenhower Comprehension Questions

Read the essay in *Growing Up to Be President*, then answer the questions below.

1. **Comprehension** Why might young Dwight's military ideas have been disregarded by his superiors, despite the excuse they gave?

   ____

   ____

2. **Knowledge** What operation did Dwight Eisenhower lead that gained him hero status and the presidency?

   ____

   ____

3. **Knowledge** What international conflict arose immediately after World War II ended?

   ____

   ____

4. **Comprehension** Explain why people might have thought that Senator McCarthy was going too far with his accusations.

   ____

   ____

5. **Application** What might life today be like if highways had never been built?

   ____

   ____

> **Word Workout**
>
> - If *euphoria* could describe a national feeling after a war, what might *euphoria* mean? Are there clues in the text that could help you?
>
> - How might someone in an argument display venomous behavior?
>
> - *Proxy* refers to someone or something that is representing something, or someone else. So what could the phrase *proxy war* mean?

John F. Kennedy Comprehension Questions

Read the essay in *Growing Up to Be President*, then answer the questions below.

1. **Knowledge** What challenge did John F. Kennedy face his whole life, that he kept secret for the sake of his political career?

2. **Knowledge** How did JFK win the presidency?

3. **Evaluation** Why do you think he might have wanted to enlist in the armed forces, despite his poor health?

4. **Evaluation** What do you think was the crew's job on a torpedo-scouting boat?

5. **Synthesis** What in JFK's background might have made him particularly suited to work on the Foreign Relations Committee?

Word Workout

- How might you invoke your classmates for help on a project?

- What do you think *chronic* means? How can clues in the text help you figure it out?

The Vietnam War

The Cold War was characterized largely by the United States fighting against the spread of communism. The U.S. goal was containment, or through threats and support for weaker countries, to keep communism from spreading. Anti-communist messaging was abundant at home, and the United States also acted overseas to halt the progress of the communist ideology.

One of the longest conflicts spurred by the policy of containment was the Vietnam War. The nation of Vietnam was split into two opposing factions: North Vietnamese, who were attempting a communist revolution; and South Vietnamese, who had a more Westernized vision for the country. The United States got involved in a limited aspect at first, sending military advisors and a small number of troops to support the South. But the conflict slowly grew in scale as the South Vietnamese government ran rampant with corruption and incompetence.

From Harry Truman to Richard Nixon, the Vietnam War was the longest war in U.S. history up until that point. Americans supported the war at first, because of the so-called domino theory—that is, if one country were to become communist, those around it might soon follow. However, as the war dragged on, many Americans protested. As more troops were sent to active duty in Vietnam, American casualties increased. This, combined with uncensored media coverage of the war, turned the tide of public opinion against the war. The government was pressured to leave Vietnam. Shortly after the U.S. withdrew, the North Vietnamese government ignored the peace treaties and quickly took control of the South.

Close Reading and Careful Speaking

1. What two groups were fighting in Vietnam?

    ____

    ____

2. What was the main reason that the United States got involved in the Vietnam War?

    ____

    ____

3. In the end, who won the Vietnam War?

    ____

    ____

Lyndon B. Johnson Comprehension Questions

Read the essay in *Growing Up to Be President*, then answer the questions below.

1. **Application** Show how Lyndon B. Johnson's upbringing affected his political priorities.

   ____

   ____

   ____

2. **Knowledge** Given the suddenness of Johnson's promotion to the presidency, what promise did Johnson make to the American people, when he was sworn into office?

   ____

   ____

   ____

3. **Knowledge** What were some of the features of Johnson's "Great Society"?

   ____

   ____

   ____

4. **Synthesis** Explain why the seemingly endless Vietnam War conflicted with Johnson's idea of a "Great Society."

   ____

   ____

   ____

Word Workout

How can you use context clues to figure out what *succumbed* means?

Richard M. Nixon Comprehension Questions

Read the essay in *Growing Up to Be President*, then answer the questions below.

1. **Knowledge** What Senate committee did Nixon serve on that was led by Joseph McCarthy?

   ____

   ____

   ____

2. **Knowledge** What campaign style did Nixon use?

   ____

   ____

   ____

3. **Comprehension** Why did the events at the end of Nixon's presidency increase the public's distrust in the government?

   ____

   ____

   ____

4. **Evaluation** Consider the actions Nixon took in his political career. What do you think he thought about his relationship with the public?

   ____

   ____

   ____

> **Word Workout**
> - If spies infiltrate a government department, why might we be worried about that?
> - Can you think of a synonym for the word *tactics*?

Gerald R. Ford Comprehension Questions

Read the essay in *Growing Up to Be President*, then answer the questions below.

1. **Knowledge** What was unique about the way Gerald Ford came into the offices of both Vice President and President of the United States?

____

____

____

2. **Knowledge** What were some of the challenges Ford faced during his term as president?

____

____

____

3. **Synthesis** How might Ford's childhood have prepared him to deal with his damaged reputation after pardoning Nixon?

____

____

____

4. **Evaluation** Although many of his plans were unsuccessful, and his term was short, today, historians tend to give Ford credit for being honest and doing his best. Do you think he should be evaluated more on his efforts or his results? Why or why not?

____

____

____

Word Workout

- Would you want your home sports team to rout their opponents?

- One of the word roots for controversial is *contra,* meaning *against*. How can this help you learn what *controversial* means?

James E. Carter Comprehension Questions

Read the essay in *Growing Up to Be President*, then answer the questions below.

1. **Knowledge** What made Jimmy Carter unique among other southern politicians, and at what point in his life did he become this way?

____

____

____

2. **Knowledge** What was the relationship Carter had with Congress, and why was it that way?

____

____

____

3. **Comprehension** In what ways did Jimmy demonstrate talents as a businessman, long before he became President?

____

____

____

4. **Evaluation** Beginning in Carter's childhood, how did he seem to be willing to take great risks?

____

____

____

> **Word Workout**
>
> - Do you know anyone who might be described as feisty? Can you describe that person?
>
> - Is there an amusement park ride that could be described as plummeted?

Ronald Reagan and the Labor Movement

	Ronald Reagan and the Labor Movement
1894	• The Pullman railroad car company cut worker pay yet forced employees to live in a company town with fixed rent. • 250,000 railroad workers went on strike. Rioting started, and when the strike ended, they had no increase in wages.
1912	• 25,000 women textile workers protested a pay cut. • Congress invited testimony on the dangerous working conditions, forcing the owners to the bargaining table. • The strikers won an overall 15% increase in pay, and a promise not to retaliate against the strikers.
1936	• United Auto Workers sat down on the factory floor, to prevent the company from hiring replacements. • For 44 days, they camped out, until the company struck a deal giving the workers a major victory.
1965	• For 5 years, California farm workers marched for better pay. • They earned better pay and a new law that gave farm workers legal bargaining power.
1968	• Memphis' 1,300 trash collectors walked off the job to demand better pay and sick leave. • After 40,000 people marched through the streets, they won a raise, and the city recognized their union.
1981	• PATCO union, air traffic controllers, stopped contract negotiations. President Reagan demanded they return to work, citing a law prohibiting government workers to strike. • Only 10% obeyed, and the President fired over 11,000 strikers, permanently breaking the union.

Info Graphic

Ronald Reagan Comprehension Questions

Read the essay in *Growing Up to Be President*, then answer the questions below.

1. **Comprehension** What can you conclude about young Ronald's character from his work as a lifeguard?

   ____

   ____

2. **Synthesis** Can you trace a thread through young Ronald's childhood experiences, to his college years, that might have led to his focus on the economy as President?

   ____

   ____

3. **Comprehension** Explain what "trickle-down" economics is and why Reagan might have thought it would lead to more jobs.

   ____

   ____

4. **Application** Ronald Reagan had been president of the actors' union, the Screen Actors' Guild. So why do you think he was not sympathetic to the PATCO strike (Professional Air Traffic Controllers Organization)?

   ____

   ____

5. **Evaluation** Reagan was a man of compromise. So why might you think he refused to compromise in his tough stand against the Soviet Union?

   ____

   ____

> **Word Workout**
> - If you theorize about what might be on a test, what exactly are you doing?
> - What might you do as a deterrent against a bully?

The Berlin Wall

Nearing the end of World War II, the Allies met to create a plan for supervising the reconstruction of Germany and ensuring that no Nazi remnants remained in power. Eventually, the Allies split Germany into occupation zones, with the Soviets taking the Eastern lands and Britain, France, and the United States dividing the West. Since the capital Berlin is in the East, they decided to split the city the same way they split the country. Once the reconstruction was completed, the occupation was supposed to end. The Soviet Union, however, decided not to leave as promised.

For several years, around two million East Germans left for the West, many of whom were skilled workers, young people, and intellectuals. The Soviet government in East Berlin finally decided to close the border to keep their people from fleeing. Overnight, barbed wire was placed along the border of East and West Berlin and was soon replaced by a high concrete wall. During the decades of living behind the wall, over 100 people were killed trying to escape from East Berlin.

Americans supported West Berlin, located deep within East Germany, and politicians often visited to show their support. President John. F. Kennedy visited and delivered a famous speech in which he said, "All free men, wherever they may live, are citizens of Berlin. And therefore, as a free man, I take pride in the words, *Ich bin ein Berliner.*" Translated, it means, "I am a Berliner." It was twenty more years until the wall would be torn down, soon after President Ronald Reagan gave a speech challenging Gorbachev, then the president of the Soviet Union, to "tear down this wall." The country would be officially re-unified shortly afterward.

Close Reading and Careful Speaking

1. What purpose did the Allies have for their meeting near the end of World War II?

   ____

   ____

2. Where is the capitol city Berlin located?

   ____

   ____

3. Why might East Berliners have wanted to live in West Berlin?

   ____

   ____

George H. W. Bush Comprehension Questions

Read the essay in *Growing Up to Be President*, then answer the questions below.

1. **Knowledge** What branch of the military did George H. W. Bush serve in?

   ____

   ____

   ____

2. **Knowledge** What problem did President H. W. Bush encounter right after taking office, and what did he do about it?

   ____

   ____

   ____

3. **Comprehension** Why was the international condemnation of Iraq's invasion of Kuwait significant?

   ____

   ____

   ____

4. **Application** What political stance did George H. W. Bush take as a congressman that might have hinted at his abilities as President to compromise with both parties in Congress, as well as other countries?

   ____

   ____

   ____

Word Workout

- When have you used a term of endearment to describe someone?

- If the economy is the balance between shoppers and stores, and between customers and businesses, then what do you suppose *economics* means?

William J. Clinton Comprehension Questions

Read the essay in *Growing Up to Be President*, then answer the questions below.

1. **Knowledge** What set of events led to the picture being taken with Kennedy, which was called prophetic of Clinton's future?

   ____

   ____

2. **Knowledge** How successful was Clinton's first term as governor of Arkansas, and how did he manage afterwards?

   ____

   ____

3. **Synthesis** What childhood circumstances might have led to his middle-of-the-road politics?

   ____

   ____

4. **Analysis** What advantages might being in the "middle-of-the-road" in politics have?

   ____

   ____

5. **Comprehension** List some ways that Clinton demonstrated being in the middle-of-the-road.

   ____

   ____

Word Workout

- Why do people say that when Bill Clinton shook President Kennedy's hand it was prophetic?

- As time went by, what events sullied the President's reputation?

- What might be a synonym for the word *centrist*?

George W. Bush Comprehension Questions

Read the essay in *Growing Up to Be President*, then answer the questions below.

1. **Knowledge** What did George W. Bush do in his college years that helped him gain important political experience?

   ____

   ____

   ____

2. **Knowledge** What major event happened early in Bush's term?

   ____

   ____

   ____

3. **Comprehension** What did Bush mean when he said, "we will make no distinction between the terrorists who committed these acts and those who harbor them"?

   ____

   ____

   ____

4. **Application** How is a war on terror different from other wars?

   ____

   ____

   ____

Word Workout

- How is it that bigotry is shown by having low expectations of someone?

- In what ways might a feeling, such as grief, be profound?

Patient Protection and Affordable Care Act, 2010

One of the struggles many American citizens have experienced over the years is the lack of healthcare, which was largely privatized, meaning private, for-profit companies provided all the services. Politicians and the public hotly debated the need for a publicly funded healthcare system from the time of President Truman in 1945.

A step towards public healthcare was made by the passage of the Affordable Care Act, finally signed into law by President Obama in 2010. Before 2010, most people only had it if they worked for a company that subscribed to a plan for its employees. If someone were unemployed, self-employed, or worked for a company that didn't offer health insurance, they paid for it on their own, and in many low-income households, that wasn't feasible. The Affordable Care Act created government subsidies to help lower the cost of health care for those low-income households.

The bill, and public healthcare in general is met with some opposition. The opposing parties' concerns largely have to do with the fact that public health care comes with tax increases, since the government needs funds to provide the aid. The bill only passed after several revisions reduced its scope, and some are still trying to repeal it today.

Close Reading and Careful Speaking

1. How many years did it take for Congress to pass a law to set up a public healthcare system?

   ____

2. What is the main objection that people have toward the Affordable Care Act?

   ____

Barack H. Obama Comprehension Questions

Read the essay in *Growing Up to Be President*, then answer the questions below.

1. **Knowledge** Why did Barack Obama struggle with his identity during his childhood?

   ____

   ____

2. **Knowledge** Which city and state did Obama work most with before he became president?

   ____

   ____

3. **Analysis** Describe some of the benefits and some of the drawbacks that a "team of rivals" might have.

   ____

   ____

4. **Comprehension** What aspect of Obama's response to the Great Recession may have showed a willingness to hear both sides of an argument?

   ____

   ____

5. **Evaluate** Why might conservative politicians consider public health care to be unconstitutional?

   ____

   ____

Word Workout

- Describe one aspect of your heritage that your family celebrates.

- Describe a project that you worked on diligently. What did you do that was diligent?

- What might be some features of an integrated neighborhood?

Excerpt from President Obama's First Inaugural Address, 2009

"…Our Founding Fathers, faced with perils that we can scarcely imagine, drafted a charter to assure the rule of law and the rights of man — a charter expanded by the blood of generations. Those ideals still light the world, ….

"So let us mark this day with remembrance of who we are and how far we have traveled. In the year of America's birth, in the coldest of months, a small band of patriots huddled by dying campfires on the shores of an icy river. The capital was abandoned. The enemy was advancing. The snow was stained with blood. At the moment when the outcome of our revolution was most in doubt, the father of our nation ordered these words to be read to the people:

"Let it be told to the future world…that in the depth of winter, when nothing but hope and virtue could survive… that the city and the country, alarmed at one common danger, came forth to meet [it]."

"America: In the face of our common dangers, in this winter of our hardship, let us remember these timeless words. With hope and virtue, let us brave once more the icy currents, and endure what storms may come. Let it be said by our children's children that when we were tested[,] we refused to let this journey end, that we did not turn back nor did we falter; and with eyes fixed on the horizon and God's grace upon us, we carried forth that great gift of freedom and delivered it safely to future generations."

Close Reading and Careful Speaking

1. President Obama mentioned "the father of our nation." Whom was he referring to?

____

____

Word Workout

Describe what might happen if someone were to falter.

Donald J. Trump

Read the essay in *Growing Up to Be President*, then answer the questions below.

1. **Knowledge** Donald Trump's father said he was a "pretty rough fellow when he was small." What was his father's solution?

2. **Knowledge** What crisis came about during the last year of Trump's term?

3. **Analysis** What aspects of Trump's brand image helped him win the presidency?

4. **Synthesis** Why might the appointing of so many conservative judges to the Supreme Court have such a long-lasting impact on the judicial system?

Word Workout

- Name a commercial product brand that you trust. What about it makes you trust it?

- How does the text help you know whether bankruptcy was a good thing or a bad thing for the Trump family?

- Find a smaller word inside *reconfiguration*. How does it help you understand the word *reconfiguration*?

Discussion Guide Answer Key

From George Washington to the Hebrew Congregation in Newport, Rhode Island, p. 2

1. George Washington wrote this letter in response to the Hebrew Congregation being unsure if they would be granted religious freedom in the new world.

2. The letter was written in 1790 after Washington received a letter from the Hebrew Congregation in Newport, Rhode Island.

3. The Hebrew Congregation may have had concerns about religious freedoms because they were in a religious minority. Religious freedom was a new concept, and they wanted assurance that the concept would extend to non-Christian religions as well.

4. Washington says that, "For happily the Government of the United States, which gives to bigotry no sanction, to persecution no assistance requires only that they who live under its protection should demean themselves as good citizens, in giving it on all occasions their effectual support." Bigotry would not be supported, and the Jews would be free to live side by side with the Christians and work together toward the common good.

5. Since it would be hypocritical to give freedom to only one religious group, this letter set the example that all religious groups would be free to practice their religion and that none would be discriminated against.

George Washington, p. 4

1. The death of his father meant he wouldn't have the money to go study in England.

2. Every member of the Congress voted for him both times.

3. His many misfortunes, including the death of his father, contracting smallpox, and suffering losses in the military taught him that good things can happen even after the bad and to just keep moving forward.

4. He left his family to serve as commander-in-chief, and similarly came out of retirement to be the country's first president.

5. Answers will vary but may include discussions such as the issues around slavery, states having different ideas about how the country should be run, and the government being new and inexperienced.

John Adams, p. 5

1. He was inspired by Cicero to develop a "glorious reputation."

2. He was a lawyer before he worked in government.

3. The Continental Congress used Adams' legal skills by having him serve on and chair many committees, and he worked on the Declaration of Independence.

4. Adams felt that the military, particularly the navy, needed bolstering.

5. Answers will vary but may include that he needed to find ways to repair the relationship between the people of his country and another state, as well as how to maintain neutrality when two U.S. allied nations are in conflict with each other.

John Adams Primary Source Discussion, p. 7

1. Sample answer provided: "...the Presence" seems to indicate some kind of holiness, or awesomeness. Later, Adams calls it the "Royal Presence" which might suggest that most people of the time thought of kings as being extremely holy, or extraordinary persons.

2. Subjects are people who answer to a king: They are the king's subjects. But citizens are equal among themselves and only answer to the law. Adams' remark is important because Americans used to be the King's subjects.

3. He meant that a new era, or epoch, was beginning.

4. Sample answer: King George seems friendly, and perhaps a little sad because he said he was the "last to consent to the Separation." But he is also hopeful that the two countries can remain friends.

Thomas Jefferson Primary Source Discussion, p. 9

1. They seem to be in writing. Evidence may vary. Sample provided: "Your mission has been communicated to the Ministers here..." implies that he and Lewis were not in the same place; some readers may also note that the level of detail in the third paragraph could only have been communicated in writing.

2. Jefferson instructs Lewis to "explore the Missouri river, & such principal stream of it, as, by it's course & Communication with the water of the Pacific ocean may offer the most direct & practicable water communication across this continent, for the purposes of commerce."

3. He is using the words "commercial disposition" and "commercial intercourse" meaning that he wants Lewis to talk about setting up business with the natives. Also, when he says "confer with them on the points most convenient as mutual emporiums" he wants Lewis to work out places, convenient to both groups, that could be set up as marketplaces.

4. Discussion should be rich with examples and thoughtful observations.

Thomas Jefferson, p. 10

1. Jefferson only freed Sally Hemmings' children in his will.

2. He was most recognized as a legal scholar.

3. The Louisiana Purchase was the transaction he made to secure the Western border and trade routes.

4. Answers may vary but can include discussions such as farmers having less taxes, having less interference with the way they operate, including their treatment of enslaved persons, and having more freedom to buy land.

5. The freedom Jefferson had to wander through the woods and read books likely fostered his love of learning and led him to be the scholar that he was.

What Are Checks and Balances?, p. 11

1. Executive, Legislative, and Judicial branches

2. James Madison developed and wrote the Constitution.

3. To ensure that no single branch of government becomes too powerful.

Adams and Jefferson Primary Source Discussion, p. 13

1. President James Monroe

2. Sample answer: "The slavery question will last long after President Monroe's political career, and even long after his own personal life and mine, unless I am mistaken."

3. A fire bell in the night would wake you up and would be terrifying.

James Madison, p. 12

1. The Virginia Plan was the document that eventually became the constitution.

2. Madison was sickly as a child because of his fear of the French and Indian War.

3. Madison played to his strengths by using his calm and persistent intellect to win people over to his side.

4. His work as the Secretary of State likely gave him the experience in government he needed to deal with his foreign affairs challenges as president.

5. Answers will vary but may include themes such as, living through his fear as a child, being supported by his family, having a good education, having allies that he could trust, and his many hours of preparation for each debate.

James Monroe, p. 14

1. Tensions arose between the states when Missouri and Maine both applied for statehood, the first as a state that would allow slavery and the latter that wouldn't allow slavery.

2. Historians believe he was the most qualified person to hold office because of the numerous government positions he held prior.

3. Politicians against slavery were worried that allowing Missouri to have slavery would make the other western territories want to apply as slavery-legal states as well.

4. When Missouri and Maine applied for statehood at the same time, the country erupted into arguments over the future of enslaved status in the United States.

5. The Monroe Doctrine stated that the U.S. would remain neutral in European conflicts, would not stand by if countries tried to retake former colonies in the Western Hemisphere, and would not accept any new colonization.

John Quincy Adams, p. 15

1. Adams' most impactful positions were the Secretary of State and Senator for Massachusetts.

2. His travels with his Father to Europe most likely gave him the worldly sense he needed to be successful with his foreign policy endeavors.

3. Adams was a strong proponent for the abolishment of slavery.

4. Adams might have been opposed so strongly because he was a stout abolitionist. Also his extensive foreign travel might have given him a very different point of view from other congressmen and senators.

Andrew Jackson, p. 16

1. Jackson ushered in "Jacksonian" politics, or the Age of Jacksonian Democracy.

2. The Trail of Tears was the forced removal of the Cherokee people from Georgia.

3. Jackson was controversial because of his background, politics, and demeanor. He was a new type of political figure the country hadn't seen before, and one that people either rejected or accepted.

4. The Cherokee Nation sought to claim their own right to self-government and may have hoped that the U.S. would have respected their rights.

5. To reject the Supreme Court's decision meant that President Jackson was putting the state's rights over the authority of the federal government.

Martin Van Buren, p. 17

1. Van Buren was the first president not born a British citizen.

2. Van Buren showed loyalty to Americans by fighting court cases against people who had old British claims to land.

3. He tried to get along with everyone by not ever revealing his own opinion, so people in New York decided that he was not to be trusted.

4. Van Buren believed in state supremacy.

5. Van Buren spent three years trying to convince Congress to approve a national banking system.

The Bank War, p. 18

1. George Washington signed the first charter in 1791. James Madison signed a second charter in 1814. And Martin Van Buren signed a third charter in 1840.

William Henry Harrison, p. 19

1. His first step was to quit studying medicine and join the military.

2. Perhaps he wanted renown because he was not the eldest son in his family and had no hope of inheriting familial wealth, or because his dad was renowned, he thought he should be too.

3. He became popular in the Northwest Territories by reducing the size of the land families could buy from the government and made it payable in installments.

4. It is possible that voters saw through his desire for fame and didn't like him.

5. Harrison's arrogance and ego might have been his fatal flaw.

John Tyler, p. 20

1. The wealth and status of his father was likely what paved the way for Tyler to have a successful career.

2. Tyler always voted with those who opposed a strong central government.

3. John Tyler set the precedent that in the event of the death of the president, the vice president would be sworn into office.

4. Tyler's unpopularity gave an opportunity for the first ever congressional overturn of a veto, and allowed Congress to try to impeach the President for the first time.

5. Congress showed that the president isn't all-powerful while Tyler was in office.

James K. Polk, p. 21

1. Polk was very close with Andrew Jackson who were both from Tennessee.

2. Polk and Jackson both supported states' rights to decide about slavery for themselves, they both grew up in the south, and were blamed for the economic depression of the late 1830s.

3. Polk demonstrated a willingness and ability to work very hard.

4. Polk claimed that American blood was shed during a border dispute which led to the Mexican-American war.

5. The tension between the North and the South grew because of the effects of the Mexican-American war and the rise of sectionalism.

Mini Lesson: The War of 1812, p. 22

1. Sample answer: Wars are expensive and perhaps France didn't have the money until they sold the territory.

Zachary Taylor, p. 23

1. Taylor showed humanity during his military career by respecting the Indians, showing concern for his troops, and conducting his duties in a way that would avoid the most conflict.

2. He might have kept his politics secret because they disagreed with most of his Southern neighbors. He did not think slavery should extend into the Western territories, and he thought the country needed a national banking system.

3. It may have showed that he had some sympathy for native peoples, both in the United States and elsewhere, such as in Nicaragua.

Millard Fillmore, p.23

1. He showed persistence by secretly getting a dictionary, teaching himself to read, getting away from his apprenticeship, and walking to a schoolhouse.

2. Answers will vary but might include discussion about poverty having a crushing effect on people's viewpoints. Young Millard's father might have been overwhelmed with stress and thus was perhaps unable to see Millard's desires until he was acting on them by himself.

3. Fillmore's childhood poverty may have made him interested in helping the poor. So he worked to pass laws against the imprisonment of debtors, who were usually poverty-stricken people.

4. The abolitionists didn't like the compromise of 1850 because the Fugitive Slave Act forced them to indirectly support slavery, and the South didn't like it because it let California be a free state.

Franklin Pierce, p. 24

1. Being popular and having a social life was a priority for Pierce throughout his life.

2. He was popular with the Southerners because he sympathized with them and fought against the abolitionists.

3. The arguments over slavery versus free states were so sensitive that no one could be elected if the nation knew how they really felt about these issues.

4. The Kansas-Nebraska act overturned the old Missouri Compromise. It caused fighting because it allowed individual states to vote on their own whether to allow slavery.

James Buchanan, p. 25

1. Buchanan grew up on the frontier with 10 other siblings on a trading and supply post. This likely encouraged a freedom that might have been hard to curtail in school and might have led to his rowdiness.

2. Buchanan was an ambassador to Russia and England.

3. Buchanan maintained a neutral stance on slavery, but he believed that the Constitution allowed states to make their own decisions on the matter.

4. Most congressman's opinions were well-known due to the vigorous debating that had taken place, and therefore, most of them were disliked by someone else. For Buchanan, he had an opportunity to stay "clean" in the debates and had made no enemies.

5. Buchanan secretly, and inappropriately, influenced the Supreme Court verdict on the Dredd Scott case. His actions hint at a weakness in his faith in the judicial system.

Abraham Lincoln, p. 26

1. Answers will vary but might include that it showed Lincoln to be confident and determined; also perhaps that he had intelligence outside the law books themselves that guided his judgment.

2. Lincoln's friendliness and intelligence made even people from the opposing party vote for him.

3. Lincoln challenged Douglas' idea of "popular sovereignty," or the concept that individual states had the right to settle the slavery issue for themselves.

4. Lincoln used the word "legal" to refer to rights that are expressed in the written law. He used the word "moral" to refer to rights that exist above the law; rights that can guide behavior, even if laws are violated.

5. Lincoln approached slave owners in states that had not seceded. He offered to pay them the value of their enslaved persons if they would free them, and they refused. Enslaved persons from the South were also running away to the North; and northern abolitionists and freedmen were urging him to free the slaves; so it was clear a decision had to be made.

6. Answers will vary but may include but are not limited to themes such as showing good judgement, having a strong moral compass, being friendly, having knowledge of the law, and having good crisis management skills. Students should give specific examples of Lincoln's actions that reveal these characteristics.

The National Banking System, p. 27

1. A bond allows a government to quickly raise money, in this case so they could purchase weapons and other materials to wage war.

2. There might have been distrust of other states' financial soundness.

Abraham Lincoln Primary Source Discussion, p. 29

1. He was speaking at the inauguration of his second term in office.

2. The nation was still fighting the Civil War, although it was nearing the end.

3. He was speaking not only to those physically present but also to the nation, since his speech would be printed in the newspapers.

4. He is referring to the institution of slavery, which ended before the war was over, since he had issued the Emancipation Proclamation.

5. He is saying that it might be God's will that all the wealth earned by enslavers through slavery should be spent on the war--"shall by sunk." And that every bit of punishment given to the enslaved should be returned to the enslavers through punishment by a sword. That if this all be God's will then this Biblical verse will be proven to be true: 'the judgements of the Lord are true and righteous altogether.'

6. He makes specific references to the civil war; he says that one-eighth of the population was enslaved; the ease with which he quotes the Bible feels like it's from another era; he also speaks freely about God's will.

Andrew Johnson, p. 30

1. Johnson's life on the frontier, apprenticeship, and business-owner background likely made him identify more with the working class than the aristocratic planters.

2. Johnson was left to deal with the aftermath of the civil war including southern reconstruction, after the death of Lincoln.

3. Johnson gave many pardons and allowed wealthy southerners back into political positions to appease them.

4. To the southern confederates, Johnson's actions seemed to justify their revolt by simply appeasing them and reinstating them, instead of trying to reconstruct the South under a new union authority.

Ulysses S. Grant, p. 31

1. Grant had a talent for horsemanship, which was desirable for cavalry troops. His dad secretly applied for the military academy for him. He was accepted for a free education in return for military service.

2. Grant was promoted to "General of the Armies," only the second man after George Washington to hold that post.

3. Grant's top priority after becoming president was the preservation of newly freed Americans' civil rights.

4. Grant showed consistency in his beliefs by supporting Black Americans' civil rights as well as appointing a Native American to be the Commissioner of Indian Affairs.

Rutherford B. Hayes, p. 32

1. Hayes was able to overcome his childhood challenges through the help of a loving family and hard work. His Uncle Sardis paid for him to go to a private school, and he studied hard to graduate.

2. Hayes supported the passage of the 14th amendment, giving citizenship status to the formerly enslaved, and the 15th amendment, which gave voting rights to all citizens regardless of previous condition of servitude.

3. Southerners were able to break their reconstruction promises because they had taken back control of the southern governments.

4. When Rutherford Hayes refused to leave the battlefield to campaign for a seat in Congress, he mirrored George Washington's own sense of duty to country. His community admired his attitude and elected him to Congress while he stayed on the battlefield.

James A. Garfield, p. 33

1. He first tried to leave the farm by getting a job on a canal boat. Since he kept falling off the boat, he quit and went back home. The second, more successful attempt was to get several part-time jobs and study for school.

2. He fought for the abolitionist movement and served on several influential committees, including a term as chair of the Appropriations Committee, which distributes funds to all the government departments.

3. Since he fired someone in the Port of New York who was trying to reform the job, and then appointed someone to whom he owed a political favor to, it showed that he was likely to use jobs as rewards. Historians think this may have been a sign the President Garfield might have allowed corruption in the White House.

4. Answers will vary but may include themes such as, but not limited to, Garfield was an abolitionist, he had dealings in the prior controversial election, and he was appointing people to his cabinet by favor. However, no reason would ever make it acceptable in a democracy to assassinate one's political opponents.

Jim Crow Laws and Variants, p. 34

1. In Mississippi, anyone who published an opinion that encouraged equality was fined $500.

2. New Orleans

3. New York also segregated their rail cars, but in a lawsuit argued by Chester Arthur before he became president, the company was forced to seat all persons equally.

4. Entertainment and/or social venues that were segregated were: libraries, restaurants, barbers, theaters, parks.

Chester A. Arthur, p. 35

1. Arthur was nicknamed for his love of expensive clothing, parties, and an expensive renovation to the White House. It was a surprising contrast to his upbringing as a poor minister's son.

2. Arthur was recommended for Vice President by the New York political machine.

3. Arthur signed the Pendleton Service Reform Act, a surprise since he came into politics through an appointment by a political machine.

4. Arthur's signing of the Pendleton Service Reform Act, as well as his funding for steel ocean cruisers were significant steps leading toward the creation of the modern era.

What Is a Political Machine?, p. 36

1. Since machines work automatically, the name seems to fit what political machines did.

2. They controlled politicians by threatening to take away their positions.

3. They were mainly trying to just stay in power. Doing good for the community was not their priority.

Grover Cleveland, p. 37

1. Cleveland put the needs of his family before his own by working when his father died instead of

going to college. His hard work allowed him to become an excellent lawyer, which gained him the reputation he needed to start a life in politics.

2. Cleveland took the attitude of a reformer to the presidency.

3. He sent the military to stop the rail strike in Chicago.

4. Perhaps historians see a reformer as someone who is only cleaning up what is before him. Whereas a visionary is someone who sees something that does not currently exist.

Benjamin Harrison, p. 38

1. His mannerisms were extremely formal and stiff.

2. He supported the Force Bill, which would have given the federal government the power to oversee elections in the South, thus protecting newly freed Black Americans' voting rights. He also spoke out against the use of force against black citizens in the South.

3. Accept all reasonable responses. He might have stayed with the law and developed a private practice, or he could have become a law professor.

William McKinley, p. 39

1. McKinley started to invite journalists to regular briefings.

2. McKinley showed his support for Black Americans by giving speeches and making appearances at black institutions.

3. McKinley was likely stopped from passing civil rights laws by Southern Democratic legislators who wanted to keep the black population oppressed.

4. He needed to decide on a standard because other countries wouldn't trade with us on a bimetal system. He chose the gold standard.

Theodore Roosevelt, p. 40

1. As a child, Teddie Roosevelt took a strong positive attitude and turned to outdoor activities to help resolve his poor health.

2. Roosevelt did not necessarily include Black Americans in his ideas of fairness.

3. Roosevelt was the first president to think the government's job was to work on behalf of the people and protect them, specifically from corporate greed.

4. By taking up economic causes for small businesses, he was opposing many in Congress who supported big business. Roosevelt relied on his extroverted nature to bring awareness to the public, and thus pressure on Congress.

5. His exercise habits and his world travels with his parents may have given him a sense of ownership about the world. This may have contributed to his eagerness to form and lead the Rough Riders.

Theodore Roosevelt National Parks and Monuments, p. 41

1. Yosemite National Park, founded in 1846

2. Arizona and Wyoming each have three monuments. But if you count monuments that became national parks, Arizona has five.

3. He established four parks in the West: North and South Dakota, Oklahoma, Colorado.

William Howard Taft, p. 42

1. His wife wanted Taft to have a political career, and his lack of interest showed in the way he approached everything as a judge rather than a politician.

2. Taft exercised his judicial expertise to help the Philippine people develop their democratic government documents.

3. Taft promised to continue in Roosevelt's footsteps, which he did not do.

4. The Republican party was so divided about Taft that Roosevelt came back to run for a third term and split the vote, which gave Woodrow Willson the election.

The Federal Reserve Act, 1913, p. 43

1. They were afraid that they would not be able to get their money back, so they took it out before the bank failed.

2. Too many financial panics would create an atmosphere in which businesses could not survive. For the economic health of the nation, Congress needed to make reforms that would create calm in the business world.

3. It's a little like trusting the fox to guard the hen house. People would not assume that bankers would fix the problem in a way that would benefit the public and not themselves.

Woodrow Wilson, p. 44

1. Answers may vary. Watching his mother nurse wounded Confederate soldiers might have instilled in him a lifelong sympathy for his Southern heritage, which showed when he instituted segregation into the federal government.

2. He surprised the political bosses by not being easy to control like they thought he would be.

3. President Wilson brought segregation from the South into the federal government by encouraging departments to "reduce friction." He also approved the requirement that applicants for jobs had to attach photos to their applications.

4. The Espionage and Sedition Act made it illegal to criticize the government or the war effort. It was unpopular because it violated freedom of speech.

5. Willson addressed Congress, something that had not been done since John Adams was President. It made the President a partner in the legislative process.

6. Willson created the draft, "meatless Mondays", daylight savings time, and signed the Espionage and Sedition Act, all to help the war effort.

The Cost of World War I, p. 45

1. If our allies have enough weapons and supplies, then the stress on our own troops is a little less.

2. Selling thousands of inexpensive stamps was a way for lower-income Americans to participate in the war effort. It raised patriotic feelings, and some money, and boosted morale on the home front.

Warren G. Harding, p. 46

1. Harding's acquisition of the Marion Star newspaper made politicians take note of his unbiased reporting style.

2. His friendly temperament and desire for popularity was one of Harding's best and worst qualities. It made him likable and therefore electable, but it also made him a poor judge of character. Thus, his cabinet was full of corrupt individuals.

3. Harding's presidency is remembered most for corruption and lack of presidential vision.

4. Hiring his friends for his cabinet may have suggested that he did not realize the difficulty of the work that they were expected to carry out. And the fact that he spoke about civil rights but didn't support the laws around them is another way in which he treated the presidency as ceremonial.

Calvin Coolidge, p. 47

1. Coolidge took a calm attitude toward the presidency. He did not believe in using the presidency as a platform for political activism, as shown by his slogan, "Keep Cool with Coolidge."

2. In response to the strike, Coolidge said, "There is no right to strike against the public safety by anyone, anywhere, anytime."

3. Coolidge was likely inspired by his Father's strong example of hard work and public service.

4. Coolidge took a much more active role in his state-level positions than he did with the presidency, as when he intervened to stop the police strike while he was Governor of Massachusetts.

Herbert Hoover, p. 48

1. Hoover was the Director of the Food Administration and Secretary of Commerce before becoming president. He also served as a diplomat to the World War I peace conference.

2. The Great Depression began during Hoover's term.

3. Answers will vary. Perhaps not; suffering often nurtures compassion.

4. Historians believe Hoover was not a great politician because he was a humanitarian and didn't fully understand government processes to inspire effective legislation.

Statistics on the Great Depression, p. 49

1. The work-relief program offered Americans about 7-8 work days per month.

2. In April 1934, about 1,100,00 Americans got work through the federal program. By January of 1935, about 2,400,000 were working. So the program employed about 1,300,000 more workers from April '34 to January '35.

3. About 33% of those employed worked in highway construction.

4. Most Americans in the program were employed in "construction and improvement of public property other than highways."

5. This 4% sector might refer to the distribution of emergency food rations, and the administration of a food stamp program.

Franklin Delano Roosevelt, p. 50

1. His distant cousin, Theodore Roosevelt, greatly inspired FDR to launch a life of public service as a politician.

2. FDR was about 39 years old when he contracted polio.

3. To restore the jobs that people had lost, the American economy needed to have a sound banking system, so that businesses could stay open and keep people working. FDR was trying to re-establish trust and hope in the American people.

4. Both FDR and his cousin Theodore believed that government should be used to protect and enhance the public good.

5. The country might not have been ready for involvement in World War II and might have been slower to respond to the global threat. Thus, the country might have been in great danger.

6. Calvin Coolidge spoke to Americans during the Jazz Age, a time of happiness and prosperity, so listeners were not in great need for comfort. Whereas, the Great Depression had created a great need among Americans and FDR happened to be an optimistic person. The combination made his Fireside Chats memorable.

FDR and World War II, p. 51

1. Sample Answer: The shock in the nation might have been even worse than it was from the attack; or the country might not have been nearly ready enough to start making weapons and munitions.

2. At that time, the head of the Japanese government was an Emperor.

3. The President is asking Congress to declare war on Japan.

Harry S. Truman, p. 52

1. His experience in farming and business school developed his management skills, which helped him in his military career, where he refined his leadership skills. Both management and leadership abilities supported his civil service work.

2. Truman ended World War II by dropping atomic bombs on Hiroshima and Nagasaki.

3. Historians have begun to appreciate the difficulties that Truman faced and have recognized his efforts to further the civil rights movement.

4. Answers will vary, but might include themes such as, the dropping of the atomic bomb, having taken over after the beloved FDR died, or his strong support of civil rights.

Dwight D. Eisenhower, p. 53

1. Pride on the part of his superiors might have caused them to reject a young soldier's ideas.

2. Eisenhower was the commander of Operation Overlord, or D-Day , the invasion of France that brought World War II to an end in Europe.

3. Rising tensions between the Soviet Union and the West gave rise to the Cold War after World War II ended.

4. McCarthy was accusing too many people without ever presenting evidence for his accusations.

5. It would be much more difficult to move goods and people to the far reaches of the country without highways.

John F. Kennedy, p. 54

1. Kennedy dealt with chronic illnesses his whole life.

2. JFK won the election by presenting a vision for the future and winning the support of black voters due to his desire to help the civil rights movement.

3. Since his father was an ambassador, and his grandfather had been a mayor, he grew up with an example of public service. So, it might have just felt natural to him to serve his country.

4. The crew was probably charged with scanning the ocean for torpedoes, or bombs traveling through the water, aiming for American ships.

5. He had lived abroad in London while his dad was the U.S. Ambassador to England, and he had written a bestselling book about England's war preparations.

The Vietnam War, p. 55

1. The North and South Vietnamese were fighting against each other.

2. The U. S. became involved because they wanted to contain the spread of communism, and because of the domino theory, they feared that countries would fall, one-at-a-time, to communism.

3. In the end, North Vietnam won the war.

Lyndon B. Johnson, p. 56

1. His poor upbringing led to a passion for development and education, which he implemented in many of the laws he supported.

2. Johnson promised to follow in JFK's footsteps and expand on his ideas.

3. Johnson created programs and supported laws that helped the poor and underdeveloped areas of the country and signed civil rights legislation, as well as continued the project to land on the moon. He also signed laws to protect the environment and to support consumer rights.

4. The war in Vietnam spent a lot of money that could have gone to developing the country instead. Never-ending conflict would naturally interfere with social progress.

Richard M. Nixon, p. 57

1. Nixon served on the House Un-American Committee.

2. Nixon used a smear campaign style, which meant that he avoided talking about political issues, and instead, he just published suspicious news about his opponent, whether or not it was true.

3. Nixon's repeated lies and attempted coverups, as well as his apparent ability to manipulate public opinion, made the public lose a significant amount of trust in the government.

4. Answers vary. Nixon may have thought of the public as tools to further his own agenda; or he might have been afraid of letting the public get to know him.

Gerald R. Ford, p. 58

1. Ford was the only president and vice president to come into both offices without being elected to either one.

2. Ford faced a damaged reputation, economic crisis, foreign policy challenges, and a congress opposed to him.

3. Answers vary. His honest and hard-working attitude in everything he did when he was young may have prepared him to make the best of a bad situation when he became president.

4. Answers will vary. Guide children to consider circumstances surrounding any effort to fix problems.

James E. Carter, p. 59

1. Carter was a liberal Democrat, who supported desegregation and rights for Black Americans. He seemed to have always had these values, even in his early years as a young businessman when he refused to joint and all-white business council.

2. Carter did not get along with his Congress, partly because he opposed pork barrel projects, which congressmen relied on for their districts.

3. Young Jimmy saved money and bought houses to rent during the Great Depression. As a young man, he also took over and saved his father's business. Carter did not waver in his support for civil rights and fought for them his whole career.

4. He seemed unafraid to take the family goods to market; he volunteered for the most dangerous work in the Navy and turned out to be on the leadership team for nuclear submarines. He was not afraid to stand apart from other white Southerners, as when he refused to support their all-white business council, and when he voted to desegregate his Baptist church.

The Berlin Wall, p. 62

1. They had to plan what to do with Germany and how to help it recover from the war.

2. Berlin is in the Eastern half of Germany.

3. Sample answer: Perhaps they had family in the western part of the city. They might not have liked the Soviet government.

Ronald Reagan, p. 61

1. Answers will vary. We might conclude that he was a risk taker, since he was a lifeguard for a dangerous river. He also must have had some physical strength to swim against currents that had trapped others.

2. Young Ronald's Dad had worked in the Works Progress Administration during the Depression, helping people find employment. Moreover, growing up during the Depression might have led him to major in economics at Eureka College. Together, these experiences may have led to President Reagan's interest in the economy.

3. Trickle-down economics is the theory that by cutting taxes for businesses, they would have more money to create jobs.

4. Sample answer: He might have thought they were putting the country in danger.

5. Answers will vary, but may include any idea about national security, or loyalty to the American ideal of capitalism and to U.S. allies.

George H. W. Bush, p. 63

1. George H. W. Bush served in the navy as a pilot.

2. President H. W. Bush inherited a huge government debt from Reagan administration.

3. The international condemnation was significant because the agreement between previous Cold War enemy powers signified the end of the Cold War.

4. George H. W. Bush's stance as a Southerner who supported Johnson's civil rights bills may been a hint that he could compromise with in Congress as President, and work with other countries in forming the coalition that fought against Iraq.

William J. Clinton, p. 64

1. Clinton was encouraged by his high school principal to follow his dreams of public service, and attended a Boy's Nation conference in Washington D.C., which allowed him to shake Kennedy's hand.

2. His first term as Governor of Arkansas did not go well, but he learned from his mistakes and served several more terms afterwards.

3. The fact that he grew up with strong women who argued often might have developed his ability to see positive points on both sides of an argument.

4. Being in the middle of the road would make it easier to compromise with the other party, temper extremists on one's own side, and potentially win more votes.

5. His speeches promoted centrist politics; he influenced other party members, and his support of Republican-led programs all demonstrated how Clinton practiced being in the middle of the road.

George W. Bush, p. 65

1. Bush helped his father with an unsuccessful senate campaign.

2. The terrorist attacks on 9/11 were the major events that happened early in Bush's presidency.

3. He meant that the United States would fight against any country that openly protected terrorist groups.

4. Wars had all previously been fought directly against known enemy countries. "Terror," or terrorist groups, did not have national affiliations, so it would be difficult to find and fight them.

Patient Protection and Affordable Care Act, p. 66

1. It took 65 years.

2. It comes with increased taxes.

Barack H. Obama, p. 67

1. He grew up apart from his black heritage, being raised in Hawaii with white grandparents.

2. Obama did most of his political work in Chicago, Illinois before becoming president.

3. Answers vary. While it may be useful, and a show of good faith, to hear both sides of an argument, it may end up slowing or stopping progress. One person would have to be the decision-maker.

4. Although Obama was in the Democratic party, he kept the Republican President Bush's plan and added to it.

5. Conservative politicians may believe the federal government shouldn't be involved in healthcare, and that it should be left up to each individual state to decide for themselves how to handle the issue.

Excerpt from President Obama's First Inaugural Address, 2009, p. 68

1. General George Washington

Donald J. Trump, p. 69

1. Trump's father sent him to a military academy to instill some discipline.

2. The COVID-19 pandemic broke out during the last year of Trump's term.

3. He portrayed himself as a successful businessman, which people trusted since they likely want successful people to run the country.

4. Since judges on the Supreme Court have lifetime appointments, they will be able to make changes to the way the law is interpreted for the rest of their lives.

Discussion Guide Bibliography

George Washington Letter to the Jewish Congregation

Washington, George. "To the Hebrew Congregation in Newport, Rhode Island." The National Archives. August 18, 1790. https://founders.archives.gov/documents/Washington/05-06-02-0135.

John Adams and King George

Adams, John. "Audience With King George III, 1785." The National Archives. June 2, 1785. https://www.archives.gov/exhibits/eyewitness/html.php?section=19.

The Bank War

The National Archives. "Conflict With the Executive: The Bank War." Accessed May 27, 2023. https://www.archives.gov/exhibits/treasures_of_congress/text/page9_text.html.

Hill, Andrew T. "The First Bank of the United States." Federal Reserve History. December 4, 2015. https://www.federalreservehistory.org/essays/first-bank-of-the-us.

Hill, Andrew T. "The Second Bank of the United States." Federalreservehistory.org. December 5, 2015. https://www.federalreservehistory.org/essays/second-bank-of-the-us.

O'Keefe, Kieran J. "Alexander Hamilton." Mount Vernon. Accessed May 27, 2023. https://www.mountvernon.org/library/digitalhistory/digital-encyclopedia/article/alexander-hamilton/#:~:text=Alexander%20Hamilton%20was%20a%20founding,of%20the%20American%20financial%20system.

Silbey, Joel. "Martin Van Buren: Domestic Affairs." Miller Center of Public Affairs, University of Virginia. Accessed May 27, 2023. https://millercenter.org/president/vanburen/domestic-affairs.

Checks and Balances

Florida A&M University Libraries. "The Sources of Federal Law: The System of Checks and Balances." Accessed June 2, 2023. https://library.famu.edu/c.php?g=276237&p=1841176#:~:text=The%20Judicial%20branch%20can%20declare,in%20whole%20or%20in%20part.

Primary Sources John Q. Adams and Thomas Jefferson React to the Missouri Compromise

Adams, John Quincy. "JQA Diary, Volume 31." John Quincy Adams Digital Library. January 10, 1820. https://www.masshist.org/publications/jqadiaries/index.php/document/jqadiaries-v31-1820-01-10-p240#sn=1.

Jefferson, Thomas. "Letter from Thomas Jefferson to John Holmes, April 22, 1820. Preserving the Union, Pt 1." U.S. Capitol Visitor Center. April 22, 1820. https://www.visitthecapitol.gov/artifact/letter-thomas-jefferson-john-holmes-april-22-1820#:~:text=In%20this%20foreboding%20letter%2C%20former,nation%20in%20violence%20and%20destruction.

Lincoln, Abraham. "Second Inaugural Address." National Parks Service. March 4, 1865. https://www.nps.gov/linc/learn/historyculture/lincoln-second-inaugural.htm.

The War of 1812

Heidler, David S. and Heidler, Jeanne T. "War of 1812." Encyclopedia Britannica. Last Modified July 2, 2023. https://www.britannica.com/event/War-of-1812#ref261171.

Onuf, Peter. "Thomas Jefferson: Foreign Affairs." Miller Center of Public Affairs, University of Virginia. Accessed June 3, 2023. https://millercenter.org/president/jefferson/foreign-affairs.

Stagg, J.C.A. "James Madison: Foreign Affairs." Miller Center of Public Affairs, University of Virginia. Accessed June 3, 2023 https://millercenter.org/president/madison/foreign-affairs.

National Banking System

Federal Reserve History. "National Banking Acts of 1863 and 1864." July 31, 2022. https://www.federalreservehistory.org/essays/national-banking-acts.

Jim Crow Laws

CBS News. "The Civil Rights Act of 1964: A Long Struggle for Freedom." Library of Congress. Accessed July 26, 2023. https://www.loc.gov/exhibits/civil-rights-act/multimedia/atlanta-schools.html.

Dobrasko, Rebekah. "Separate But Equal? South Carolina's Fight Over School Segregation (Teaching with Historic Places.)" National Parks Service. Last modified May 17, 2023. https://www.nps.gov/articles/separate-but-equal-south-carolina-s-fight-over-school-segregation-teaching-with-historic-places.htm.

Harvey, Gordon. "Public Education in Alabama After Desegregation." Encyclopedia of Alabama. Last modified March 27, 2023. https://encyclopediaofalabama.org/article/public-education-in-alabama-after-desegregation/.

Library of Congress. "School Segregation and Integration." Accessed July 26, 2023. https://www.loc.gov/collections/civil-rights-history-project/articles-and-essays/school-segregation-and-integration/.

National Parks Service. "Jim Crow Laws." Last modifies April 17, 2018. https://www.nps.gov/malu/learn/education/jim_crow_laws.htm.

Urofsky, Melvin I. "Jim Crow Law." Encyclopedia Britannica. Last modified July 21, 2023. https://www.britannica.com/event/Jim-Crow-law.

Political Machine

The Editors of Encyclopedia Britannica. "Political Machine." Encyclopedia Britannica. Last modified September 19, 2022. https://www.britannica.com/topic/political-machine/additional-info#history.

Theodore Roosevelt National Parks and Monuments

National Parks Service. "Theodore Roosevelt and Conservation." Last modified November 16, 2017. https://www.nps.gov/thro/learn/historyculture/theodore-roosevelt-and-conservation.htm.

The Federal Reserve Act, 1913

Moen, Jon R and Tallman, Ellis W. "The Panic of 1907." Federal Reserve History. December 4, 2015. https://www.federalreservehistory.org/essays/panic-of-1907.

Richardson, Gary and Romero, Jessie. "The Meeting at Jekyll Island." Federal Reserve History. December 4, 2015. https://www.federalreservehistory.org/essays/jekyll-island-conference.

Richardson, Gary and Sablik, Tim. "Banking Panics of the Gilded Age." Federal Reserve History. December 4, 2015. https://www.federalreservehistory.org/essays/banking-panics-of-the-gilded-age#:~:text=Between%201863%20and%201913%2C%20eight,1907%20spread%20throughout%20the%20nation.

Great Depression Graphic

Federal Government. "Emergency Work Relief Program of the FERA." Internet Archive. 1935. https://archive.org/details/nby_167161-4.

World War I

National Museum of the United States Air Force. "Liberty Bond and War Saving Stamps Leaflets." September, 1918. https://www.nationalmuseum.af.mil/Visit/Museum-Exhibits/Fact-Sheets/Display/Article/579630/liberty-bond-and-war-saving-stamps-leaflets/

Library of Congress. "Finances of the War." Accessed July 31, 2023. https://www.loc.gov/collections/world-war-i-rotogravures/articles-and-essays/events-and-statistics/finances-of-the-war/

Franklin Delano Roosevelt and World War II

Roosevelt, Franklin D. "Annotated Draft of Proposed Message to Congress Requesting Declaration of War Against Japan." National Archives Catalog. December 7, 1941. https://catalog.archives.gov/id/593345

Vietnam War

Spector, Ronald H. "Vietnam War." Encyclopedia Britannica. Last modified June 16, 2023. https://www.britannica.com/event/Vietnam-War/French-rule-ended-Vietnam-divided.

Berlin Wall

History.com Editors. "Berlin Wall." History.com. Last modified April 20, 2023. https://www.history.com/topics/cold-war/berlin-wall.

Kennedy, John F. "Remarks in the Rudolph Wilde Platz." John F. Kennedy Presidential Library and Museum. June 26, 1963. https://www.jfklibrary.org/asset-viewer/archives/JFKWHA/1963/JFKWHA-200-001/JFKWHA-200-001.

Morris, David. "The Rise and Fall of the Berlin Wall." Library of Congress. November 1, 2019. https://blogs.loc.gov/international-collections/2019/11/the-rise-and-fall-of-the-berlin-wall/.

The Editors of Encyclopedia Britannica. "Berlin Wall." Encyclopedia Britannica. Last modified June 30, 2023. https://www.britannica.com/topic/Berlin-Wall.

Ronald Reagan and the Labor Movement

Kiger, Patrick J. "10 Major Labor Strikes Throughout U.S. History." History, May 3, 2023. Accessed, August 3, 2023. https://www.history.com/news/strikes-labor-movement

Malone, Kenny, and Julia Simon. "Looking Back on When President Reagan Fired the Air Traffic Controllers." National Public Radio, August 5, 2021. Accessed on August 3, 2023. https://www.npr.org/2021/08/05/1025018833/looking-back-on-when-president-reagan-fired-air-traffic-controllers

Martin, Roland. "Carnegie Steel Company." Encyclopedia Britannica. Accessed on August 3, 2023. https://www.britannica.com/topic/Carnegie-Steel-Company

Schalch, Kathleen. "1981 Strike Leaves Legacy for American Workers." National Public Radio, August 3, 2006. Accessed on August 3, 2023. https://www.npr.org/2006/08/03/5604656/1981-strike-leaves-legacy-for-american-workers

Wallenfeldt, Jeff. Editor. "Henry Clay Frick: American Industrialist and Philanthropist." Encyclopedia Britannica. Accessed August 3, 2023. https://www.britannica.com/biography/Henry-Clay-Frick

Patient Protection and Affordable Care Act

U.S. Department of Health and Human Services. "About the Affordable Care Act." Accessed June 5, 2023. https://www.hhs.gov/healthcare/about-the-aca/index.html.

Excerpt's from First Inaugural Speech

Obama, President Barack Hussein Obama. "Inaugural Address." Accessed, August 3, 2023. https://obamawhitehouse.archives.gov/realitycheck/the_press_office/President_Barack_Obamas_Inaugural_Address